The Hitchhiker's Guide To Elvis

By Mick Farren

D1253504

Published by Collector's Guide Publishing, Box 62034, Burlington, Ontario, Canada, L7R 4K2

Manufactured in Canada
The Hitchhiker's Guide To Elvis / Mick Farren
First Edition
ISBN 0-9695736-5-0

To Harry Rose,
who's been a hitchhiker all his life

Contents

Don't panic!

**You are entering
the Elvis Universe.**

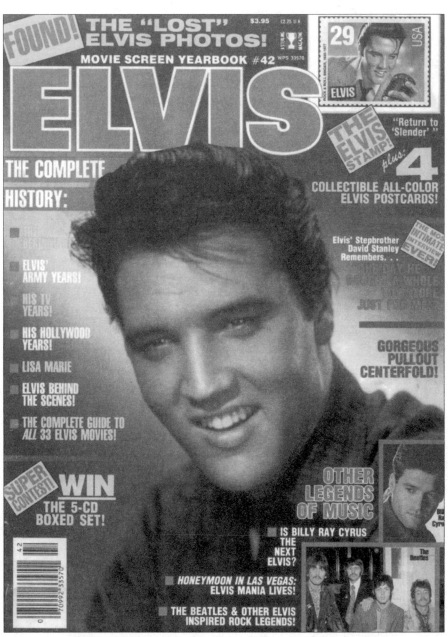

FOUND!

THE "LOST" ELVIS PHOTOS!

$3.95 £2.25 U.K

MOVIE SCREEN YEARBOOK #42 WPS 33570

29 USA
ELVIS

ELVIS

THE ELVIS STAMP!

"Return to 'Slender'"

plus 4 COLLECTIBLE ALL-COLOR ELVIS POSTCARDS!

THE COMPLETE HISTORY:

- THE BEGINNING
- ELVIS' ARMY YEARS!
- HIS TV YEARS!
- HIS HOLLYWOOD YEARS!
- LISA MARIE
- ELVIS BEHIND THE SCENES!
- THE COMPLETE GUIDE TO *ALL* 33 ELVIS MOVIES!

Elvis' Stepbrother David Stanley Remembers...

THE MOST INTIMATE INTERVIEW EVER!

THE DAY HE SOLD A WHOLE STORE JUST FOR...

GORGEOUS PULLOUT CENTERFOLD!

SUPER CONTEST!! **WIN** THE 5-CD BOXED SET!

OTHER LEGENDS OF MUSIC

Billy Ray Cyrus

- IS BILLY RAY CYRUS THE NEXT ELVIS?
- *HONEYMOON IN LAS VEGAS:* ELVIS MANIA LIVES!
- THE BEATLES & OTHER ELVIS INSPIRED ROCK LEGENDS!

The Beatles

Elvis fan magazine, published 1992—fifteen years after his death

Without Elvis, you're nothing.
—Madonna

Perspectives constantly shift, and no true sense of scale or proportion can be found. The lines that divide legend and history, truth and mythology, reality and illusion are blurred and inexact, and at times, vanish altogether. The Elvis Universe is a place where individuals are able to believe just about anything they want, and Elvis Presley can be all things to all people. It is a galaxy with but a single star and a million circling satellites. Just to complicate matters, in real time, that central star collapsed on itself back in 1977, too unstable to sustain its mass, but it is still defined by those attendant moons that are seemingly locked in permanent, never-ending orbits. To the cosmic traveler, coming upon the Elvis Universe for the very first time, it must seem like some perverse Disneyland, created and maintained by the needs, the memories, and the illusions of its strange denizens.

Unlike Disneyland, however, the Elvis Universe could never be described as the happiest place on Earth. Too many missed chances and thoughts of what might have been have turned it into a place of shadows, and the presence of death at its hollow centre can never quite be ignored. Too many ghosts and too many passed up chances of glory, and if that wasn't enough, the population is not only strange, but propelled by a variety of different motivations. On every level, one can't help but encounter legions of hustlers, hucksters, and fast buck artists who have gone into overdrive attempting to cash in on the gathering mystique that is now Elvis Presley. Equally abundant are the inadequate, the emotionally crippled, and the socially dysfunctional who have convinced themselves that their very survival depends on a set of imaginary emotional bonds with that mystique. Somewhere between the two fall the ranks of those strange individuals who strive for some kind of spurious influence and prestige in otherwise powerless lives by slavishly imitating the image of the man.

By all logical criteria, the Elvis Universe shouldn't exist at all. More than forty years have passed since the skinny eighteen-year-old walked into Sun Records and paid $3.98-plus-tax to cut a crude, double-sided acetate of the songs "My Happiness" and "That's When Your Heartaches Begin." The twenty-year benchmark rapidly approaches since the stoned and bloated forty-two-year-old died in isolated luxury with a woman whose main claim to fame was that she had, once upon a time, held the title of Memphis' "Miss Traffic Safety." According to the rules of both entropy and show business, Elvis Presley should be little more than a faded memory, or at the very most, an early entry in the Rock & Roll Hall of Fame.

His twenty-two-year career as a major recording star and movie idol blazed bright with initial glory, was rekindled in a dazzling comeback, but for the rest of the time, wallowed in dismal repetition and creative bankruptcy. The

The Boy King

disappointments far outweighed the rapture, yet those comparatively few moments were of such quantum intensity that the memory of them surpassed some critical boundary, beyond which they assumed a life of their own. Elvis the man has long gone, but the energy of Elvis the myth not only continuously regenerates itself, but seemingly grows and expands.

The concept of the Elvis Universe may sound far-fetched, but I find myself hard pressed to describe what Elvis Presley has been turned into during the years since his death in any other way. The possible alternatives that spring to mind—"mass obsession," "cult," or maybe "religion"—seem even less plausible. Yet how else can one explain both a public and private fixation that has created its own rules, mysteries, folklore, conspiracy theories, and holy relics that continues to pose seemingly endless unanswerable questions, and above all, absolutely refuses to go away? What other reason can be offered for the unbelievable volumes of merchandise that continue to pour out of factories and printworks, all the books, the recycled records and films, the images that repeat themselves seemingly to infinity, Elvis cookbooks, Elvis nightshirts, Elvis toothpick holders (I swear to god)? On the semantic level, why is it that the name "Presley" has effectively been all but dropped from the Name Of The King, and that he is known by the single name—"Elvis"?

The word universe, as used in the context that I use it here, was a term coined by comic book publishers when they decided to make all their various fantasies interlock and work together. The relationship between Superman, Batman, the Green Lantern and Wonder Woman was that they all existed in the DC Comics universe, a dimension parallel to our own, where the rules made sense, where Superman's alter-ego Clark Kent worked at the *Daily Planet* in the city of Metropolis, and Bruce Wayne's Batcave was just outside of the neighbouring Gotham City.

The comic book universe was also a place where imagination and marketing combined to provide a fantasy refuge from the stress of a less-than-perfect reality. Men could fly and leap tall buildings in a single bound; villains were ultimately vanquished and the good people ultimately saved. In the Elvis Universe, one can also find a weird kind of freedom from the pain of life. The harsh rules of logic no longer apply, and at no risk of exaggeration, Elvis can be just about anything to anyone—lover, father figure, icon, role model, even, it would seem, something approaching a deity.

The way in which the memory of Elvis can be all things to all people was nowhere more amply demonstrated than by the 1992 "election" held by the U.S. Postal Service to select the design of the Elvis commemorative 29 cent stamp. The American public was asked which of two Elvis stereotypes it preferred—the young rockabilly or the spangled showbiz idol of the Las Vegas era. In many respects, the stamp vote institutionalized a division among Elvis fans that had been developing for years.

On one side of the divide, there had always been steadfast rock & rollers, the ones who wanted to preserve the memory of the young, raw, sexually-charged Elvis, the rebel in black and shocking pink cat clothes, the hillbilly zootsuiter who challenged established standards of entertainment and many of the most cherished assumptions of the fifties. Facing them across the widening gulf were the more conventional Middle Americans who demanded a safer, more manageable Elvis who provided comfort and reliability in predictable white spangles.

The U.S. Postal Service
Elvis Presley ballot card

It almost seemed that someone at the Postal Service—perhaps an Elvis fan themselves—had realised that, although these two images were both Elvis, that was about all they had in common. In all other respects, they were virtually irreconcilable. The devotees of the young Elvis were individuals who had tended to move with the continuing forward motion of rock & roll. Among their number, they even included the rockers of later generations—Bruce Springsteen, Robert Plant, Billy Idol, even the late John Lennon, with his now legendary remark, "Before Elvis, there was nothing." They certainly viewed Elvis as the fountainhead of much of what they held dear, but they also recognised that, down the flow of time, all things adapted, mutated, grew, and changed.

Facing them across the divide, were a crowd of people for whom change was threatening, something to be avoided wherever possible. For them, Elvis, in his Vegas suit of lights performing "Love Me Tender" or "Memories," provided a constant, unchanging reference point in a world that seemed to be in such a state of flux that it had become a terrifying place. Many of these people seemed to have little or no relationship with rock & roll apart from through Elvis, and if they had any other records in their collection, they were more likely to be Barry Manilow, Wayne Newton or The Carpenters. These were the cliched Elvis fans who the media regularly held up to ridicule, and seemed to have virtually taken control of the artifacts and the memory of Elvis.

Whoever had the brainwave to stage an actual grassroots poll to determine which Elvis would grace the stamp was operating according to a very basic and very simple concept of democracy that isn't seen too often these days. All we had to do was to go to the post office in April of 1992, pick up a yellow card, check the Elvis of our choice and drop the card into a mailbox. Aside from affixing a 19 cent stamp to the card, we suffered no fuss, no muss, no electioneering, and no dirty politics.

The big surprise in the Elvis stamp "election" was that the "young Elvis" came out the winner. From observing the pilgrims at Graceland, the participants at various Elvis fan events, even the style of the greater proportion of Elvis merchandising, and the general attitude of the media, I had assumed by at least the late eighties that the memory of Elvis had pretty much been co-opted by the devotees of the Las Vegas Elvis, and those of us who still honoured the untamed rock & roller were very much in the minority. On the surface, it had looked as though the "hillbilly cat" had all but been buried by the karate moves, the ritual laying on of scarves and all the other grandiose spectacles of the seventies stage shows and the hundreds of ludicrous impersonators in side-burns and aviator sunglasses.

The fact that the vote went to the young Elvis by an easy margin was strangely comforting. It was as though a silent majority in the country still had a memory in their hearts of the pure, wild young man who turned music on its head, rather than the late-model phenomena that had strayed close to becoming a parody of himself. It also seemed to prove the layers of nonsense that had all but buried Elvis in the decade or so following his death, the tabloid fantasies that he was still alive or consorting with UFO aliens, had failed to obscure the man's real power and real impact on Western popular culture.

It also once again posed a question that had dogged music critics and social commentators since at least the early sixties. What exactly was the power of Elvis Presley, what was the unique factor that placed him above all other enter-tainers, artists, and cultural icons of the twentieth century to the point that he had become Elvis, a figure of almost supernatural proportions?

✧   ✧   ✧

My own first entry into the Elvis Universe was as a small English boy in a Southern coastal town, in his bedroom, listening to the radio. My initiation took exactly two minutes and six seconds, the time required to hear "Heartbreak Hotel" from start to finish. At the time, I had almost no interest in music. At that time, music meant Doris Day, Teresa Brewer or Perry Como. I had better things with which to occupy my time.

The airing of "Heartbreak Hotel" was on a show that I believe had the less than original title of "Hit Parade." The show was on Radio Luxembourg, an English language station broadcasting out of continental Europe that played pop music, radio game-shows, U.S. evangelists like Billy Graham and Garner Ted Armstrong, plus a handful of kid-oriented drama shows. I'd tuned my bakelite Ecko radio to Luxembourg to catch a science-fiction serial adventure called "Dan Dare, Pilot of the Future" that came on every evening at 7:15. Dan Dare lived sometime around the year 2000, and was the ace pilot of the United Nations Space Fleet. He was also featured in the comic book *Eagle*.

According to the predictions contained in Dan Dare, world peace had been achieved, atomic weapons had been outlawed in 1967, and people lived in that consumer dreamland where everyone had their own car, house, television set, microwave, and freezer, and everything was run on cheap, clean atomic power. The only price to be paid for this materialist utopia was conformity and obedi-ence to the rules. The only danger was posed by malignant aliens from beyond the Earth, and Dan Dare took care of them. Aside from these aliens, this was the future being heavily promoted all over the "free" world. It was certainly the future that they told you about in school. A clean, safe, plastic-coated, drip-dry tomorrow in which you worked hard, toed the line, conformed in dress and attitude, and eventually you'd wind up with a good job— (some nebulous office gig like the father figures on fifties TV sitcoms; in the future, the sweatshops and dark satanic mills would all be automated)—and eventually you'd get all the goodies, all the stuff, all those major appliances and consumer durables. In this world, the only fly-in-the-ointment, the only threat wasn't evil aliens, it was the Godless Communists and the fear that the Reds would start an atomic war before capitalism had made everything perfect.

Even way back then, I think I suspected that all was not quite right with the fifties dream. Although I certainly could not have voiced it, I suspect I was already subconsciously wondering when the fun came in. That was probably why I was listening to "Dan Dare, Pilot Of The Future" in the first place. The idea of a future career doing raygun battle with malignant aliens seemed, if a tad fantastic, infinitely preferable to putting on a suit and tie and going to an office day-in and day-out until I got old and died.

In two minutes and six seconds, Elvis put an end to all that. Elvis offered a whole different future. He had defined the missing fun. In the frantic, sobbing rage of "Heartbreak Hotel," he announced how an alternative actually existed to the obedience and the conformity, how we could conceivably reshape the world in our image—and his. That was the seduction, and like any red-blooded kid, I went for it. If I needed any confirmation of the power of Elvis, it came in the way in which my stepfather hated him. And I don't mean he disliked the music—it went far deeper than that. My stepfather really loathed Elvis, deeply and implacably. In one particularly nasty outburst when, in short order, I began hauling home Elvis records instead of model aircraft construction kits, he even suggested that both Elvis and myself were homosexual. In the homophobia of the fifties, this was fighting talk, just about the ultimate insult, and it clearly indicated how dangerous my old man considered Elvis to be, and just how much he feared rock & roll and everything about it. By far the easiest way to gauge a threat is to check out the fear levels of the threatened.

Of course a similar message was already being more lucid and articulately delivered by James Dean, Marlon Brando and the Beat Generation. Unfortunately, I was just a tad young for the first run of *Rebel Without A Cause;* until the late sixties, *The Wild One* was banned in the U.K., and I didn't get my hands on a copy of Allen Ginsburg's *Howl* or Jack Kerouac's *On The Road* until JFK was in the White House and Bob Dylan was trying to sound like Woody Guthrie. For me, like millions of my peers, the original spark of revolution was kindled by none other than Elvis.

✧　　　✧　　　✧

An "X" factor exists regarding Elvis. That is the one thing that isn't open to any real kind of argument. You can only go so far with virtually any facet of the Elvis Presley story before you run into something that simply doesn't make sense. You're suddenly asking yourself—how the hell could he have done that?

How could he have made a particularly ill-timed or ill-conceived career move and not alienated a serious majority of his fans? How could he make all of those god-awful records, and cut songs that were nothing short of just plain bad without the bulk of his audience walking away? How could he spend almost an entire decade of his life making all of those ludicrous movies? How could one man squander so much talent and never really be called to account for it?

A significant proportion of Elvis fans would seem to have an almost infinite capacity for forgiveness. The stunningly handsome Boy King could turn himself into a grotesquely bloated blimp, but fans would continue to worship the fountainhead, blanking out the unpleasant reality with a level of denial that, at times, appeared to verge on group psychosis. Even his death was greeted with various forms of disbelief and rejection that would eventually grow and mutate into, on one hand, the "Elvis is alive" fantasy (and all of the money-making schemes that were spawned by that bizarre concept), or on

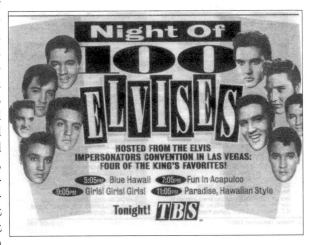

another, and if the graffiti on the wall surrounding Graceland is to be believed, the faith that—sometime, somehow—Elvis will return.

A weird selflessness is observable among the hard-core Elvis fans that is almost unique in the relationship between an entertainer and his audience. No matter how devoted, the fans of other show-business figures still maintain what might be called a transactional link with their idol. As long as the performer continues to deliver the goods, the fans will remain, but if he or she starts turning out mediocre product or vanishes from view for a protracted period of time, then the fans will start looking elsewhere for a connection that will fulfill their needs. With the Elvis fan, quite the reverse would seem to be true. To paraphrase JFK, they "ask not what Elvis can do for them, but what they can do for Elvis." On the outer extremes, one can even find characters like Kiki Apostolakos, who left her home and family in Greece to come to Graceland on a daily basis, and to otherwise devote her entire life to the singer's memory. Presented with this and other examples of what looks to be totally illogical self-sacrifice, it's little wonder that commentators like British theologian Ted Harrison are starting to talk in terms of Elvis worship as a type of developing religion. To the unbeliever, many of the established religions will also appear quite illogical.

None of this, though, answers the crucial question—how did all this get started? What is the "X" factor that caused Elvis to grow to the near-deity status that he enjoys today? As I've already suggested, the key may well be in the

initial impact. Was Elvis, on first contact, able to impart some indestructible energy to his fans that would remain with them for the rest of their lives and actually outlive the man himself?

Casting around for something that might fit this theory, the first thing we come across is rock & roll itself. Elvis may not have invented rock & roll, but he sure as hell brought it ready-packaged to a mass audience, delivered by an ultra-handsome, uninhibited, charismatic white boy.

In the full tilt, pedal-to-the-metal craziness of the sixties, a whole lot of us believed that rock & roll could change the world. Although many of us may have revised our ideas or at least reduced our expectations, Elvis certainly emerged from a world of bland and predictable pop music with something unprecedented and immensely powerful, and those of us who were there to witness it knew, without a word being said, that Elvis was talking youth revolt —he was talking the breaking down of barriers, he was talking change. His body language spoke of a new sexuality, and a refusal to conform to what had gone before. Above all, he was talking attitude.

And yet the event of rock & roll can't be the whole of the story. Or perhaps it's actually a separate story of its own, with Elvis in the beginning, but in short order, Elvis and the forward movement of rock definitely parted company. With only occasionally significant backward glances, Elvis, after he came out of the Army, pretty much turned his back on anything but the most MOR interpretations of the music. In addition, a large percentage of current Elvis fans, and even some of those in the outer twilight zone of total extremism, weren't around to fall for the rocking rebel of the mid-fifties, and didn't come to Elvis via "Heartbreak Hotel," "Mystery Train," or "Blue Suede Shoes." A large proportion of those standing in line to make the tour of Graceland, or carrying candles in the yearly parade that marks his death, are connected to the "second Elvis," the Elvis of the white jumpsuit, "Can't Help Falling In Love," and "American Trilogy." Thus the impact of rock & roll, although it is certainly a part of the power of Elvis, can't be the whole story, and we still have to look elsewhere for the secret.

Although it may sound strange, something else that might be worth looking at is the relationship that Elvis had with his audience via television. We usually think of Elvis in terms of recordings and films, and the part that TV played in his career tends to be largely ignored, except for maybe his appearance on "The Ed Sullivan Show" and the old story of how Sullivan ordered that he should be shot from the waist-up only. In fact, during 1956, when Elvis was making his big push for international stardom, he performed no less than twelve times on network TV. In later life, he also seemed to turn instinctively to television when a point had to be made or when the going got rough. He appeared as a guest of honour on the "Frank Sinatra Show" when he first got out of the Army, even though Sinatra had, just two years earlier, condemned all rock & rollers as "cretinous goons."

In 1968, when Elvis' career was at an all-time low, and all but the most myopic fans had finally admitted that his motion picture output had dropped to the level of the unwatchable, and that his records, with only a few exceptions, had sunk to almost the same wretched level, Elvis again turned to television as his big hope of salvation. He was coming home to rock & roll in a black leather suit, and the move was going to be played out in front of hundreds of millions of viewers across the world. Ratings went through the roof, and Elvis' prestige and credibility were restored in a single, prime-time hour.

TV was even used to solve the Colonel's problems. The story of the Colonel's illegal immigrant background and the fact that he was afraid to leave the U.S. because he never owned a valid passport is now such a familiar story that it hardly needs to be repeated here. In 1973, the demand that Elvis tour Japan had become so intense that Parker could no longer simply ignore it and still remain plausible as a manager. The early seventies had seen the introduction of the first worldwide

Elvis' star on the Hollywood Walk of Fame

satellite hook-ups for major boxing spectaculars that had been made possible by a combination of advancing technology and the massive global popularity of Muhammed Ali. In this, Parker saw a way off the hook. By broadcasting the live "Aloha From Hawaii" show directly to Japan at 12:30 A.M., a time that, although totally unsuitable for the continental U.S., happened to be right in the middle of Japanese prime evening viewing, he gave that vital market an approximation of their own live show and staved off his problem for a couple more years.

Elvis' first TV broadcast coincided with the first golden age of television. By 1956, TV had ceased to be a novelty and was quickly being assimilated into American family life. Most households owned a set by that time, and the behaviour patterns and even the expectations of those households was being radically altered by this newly acquired piece of electronic furniture. It was the era of the first TV mega-stars like Milton Berle, Lucille Ball and Jackie Gleason. In a weird way, Elvis could also be counted among that list. Although Elvis' TV spots were comparatively few and far between, compared to the stars who hosted or performed in their own series, when Elvis did appear on "Stage Show" or "The Ed Sullivan Show," his impact was electric and the ratings were astronomical. Elvis on TV was a significant event for millions of teenage fans, a magical moment, provided by twentieth-century magic that could place Elvis himself right in their homes, on the tiny flickering screen.

It also seemed as though Elvis has an instinctive understanding of TV. To watch the old black and white kinescopes of Elvis performing "Heartbreak Hotel" on his third Dorsey brothers "Stage Show," you see a man who knew exactly what he could do with the medium and exactly what the medium could do for him. The twitches of his hips and the small movements of his face all build to the moment of frenzy when the guitar solo cuts in. The harsh contrast of the

Elvis on the "Milton Berle Show"

early TV lighting is used to absolute effect. Elvis drops his head and his eyes become dark shadows of both threat and promise. His features are thrown into such stark relief that they assume the symmetry of a Michelangelo sculpture. You have to know that the young women of America, wrestling puberty in a time of intense sexual repression, are staring at the set, into those black holes that are Elvis' eyes, open-mouthed and breathless. A psychic/electronic link is being formed between Elvis and his audience that far transcends the limitations of the unsteady black & white picture. The older generation can also sense this link, and that's why they write letters of protest to newspapers and TV stations. That's why they bad mouth Elvis at work, and they start to wonder if this sideburned son of white trash might conceivably be the anti-Christ.

So is television the answer? Is the real secret of Elvis' initial impact that he appeared at exactly the optimum moment on what was still a revolutionary medium? Or is that just too easy?

❖   ❖   ❖

I remember very clearly the sense of betrayal we felt when Elvis went in the Army. English schoolboys, gathered around a cheap, single-speaker record player covered in blue and white vinyl, like the seats of a '58 Chevy. Too young for girls, living vicariously through the power of rock & roll, we'd get together at the home of a kid named Roy Afleck. His father played in a dance band, and was marginally more tolerant of our new found obsession than some of our parents. Roy Afleck even played the guitar.

Of course, it was no longer just a matter of Elvis. By this time, we'd progressed to Gene Vincent, Little Richard, Buddy Holly, Jerry Lee Lewis, and Chuck Berry. An affection still lingered even for Bill Haley and the Comets. Elvis remained, however, the central figure. How could it be otherwise, at that time, he was turning out music that was nothing less than magnificent. Songs like "I Want To Be Free" and "Baby, I Don't Care" throbbed with the caged lion pulse of young boy discontent. "Don't" and "One Night With You" set thoughts in motion, triggered aches that we knew most likely wouldn't be released in reality until we were at least fifteen or sixteen.

And then we heard that they were taking him away. The bastards were dragging Elvis off to the Army, symbolically shaving off his wild hair that we so longed to copy, substituting shapeless olive drab for the pink and black suits that we desperately wanted, but couldn't wear, and couldn't afford. And the whole miserable spectacle was going to be conducted in the full glare of the media so the humiliation would be total. We kids had been given a glimpse of the promised land, and then, in just a matter of a year or so, it was being canceled. Even with the limited symbolic appreciation of young boys, we knew what was going on. We knew what the highly publicised haircut meant, why every cheap-shot comedian was putting so much emphasis on it. We also lived through the haircut bullshit at school. They wanted our hair short, making us ugly and docile. We wanted it long, with pride and a DA. We suffered the detentions and the other punishments on account of the hair conflict. We knew there

Elvis' first major publicity photo

was no point in pretending, the drafting of Elvis wasn't just something that happened. It was an ancient and evil ritual. They weren't merely giving Elvis an Army fresh-fish haircut; metaphysically, they were cutting his balls off. The fearful elders were castrating the Boy King, and we were all expected to watch. Maybe it was intended as an object lesson: Give up the fight, kids; if we can get Elvis, we sure as hell can get you. Maybe it was supposed to scare us into submissive conformity. In fact, all it did was make us sullen and mean. As the *London Times* pointed out in its 1977 obituary of Elvis, "he opened the first cracks that would eventually widen into the generation gap."

We didn't know at the time that he'd end up in Bad Neuheim, Germany, living in low profile luxury with a constant supply of frauleins. As far as we were concerned, Elvis had been taken, and he was missing in an undeclared war.

For two long years we waited, tantalised by the compilation re-issues that the Colonel and RCA kept putting out and sustained by the other rockers who had followed in Elvis' wake. Despite the efforts of the BBC, Britain's state-controlled radio and TV system, to suppress it, there was no shortage of good rock & roll. Some of the older kids had even started playing it themselves. Only Elvis was missing.

The first single after Elvis emerged from the military was "Stuck On You," and it came as nothing less than a shock. It was a pleasant enough rock tune, but something was definitely lacking. Something had gone, not only from the music, but seemingly from Elvis himself. No matter how we attempted to reassure ourselves, the power was diminished. Although he redeemed himself with a uniquely powerful album, *Elvis Is Back*, there was still no way that my friends and I could pretend that the same Elvis who had gone into the Army had come back to us intact. The level of his music started to fall away. Some great rock records followed like "Mess Of Blues," "His Latest Flame," "Return To Sender," but at the same time, we had to contend with "Wooden Heart," "Bossa Nova Baby," and "It's Now Or Never," songs which seemed to indicate that the Hillbilly Cat was now pitching to be Mario Lanza. The movies told the story even more plainly. Where once there had been *Jailhouse Rock*, now we had lightweight candy floss like *G.I. Blues* or *Blue Hawaii*. Elvis had left the revolution.

The grief was for what amounted to a lost leader. Elvis had launched this rock & roll ship of fools, but then left us to navigate it ourselves while he holed up in Hollywood making idiot musicals and beach movies. Like most Elvis fans, we obviously couldn't blame Elvis himself for what was going down. The first thing you notice in the Elvis Universe is that no one ever, ever blames Elvis for anything. They had done something to Elvis in the Army. That was the best that we could come up with. The bastards had taken the exotic wild man and tamed him. That's why they'd put him on "The Frank Sinatra Show"—that's what *G.I. Blues* was supposed to demonstrate. Elvis was housebroken, and presumably, it was more reinforcement of the message that we could expect the same to happen to us by the time they were through. Although we wouldn't have used those words at the time, the castration conspiracy theory was running hot and strong.

In many respects, the way I felt about this loss of Elvis was the way, when much younger, I had first heard the New Testament story of Jesus Christ. The way the teacher had told it, the big deal at the core of Christianity was that Jesus had risen from the grave; yet, I couldn't quite bring myself to accept that Jesus had supposedly returned from the dead. He was too spectral, more like a ghost than a flesh and blood human. In both cases, Jesus and Elvis, I knew something had been taken away, no matter how many people wanted to tell me that it hadn't.

Making comparisons between Elvis Presley and Jesus Christ may seem over the top to some and downright blasphemous to others—although an irreverent cartoon book titled *Elvis and Jesus*, that was published in time for Christmas 1993, did exactly that. The fact also has to be faced that, two decades after Elvis' death, some of the most obsessive fans appear to maintain a personal relationship with their idol that is very much akin to that which born-again Christians profess to have with Jesus.

The trouble really starts when you begin to dig into these obsessions and what can only be called Elvis worship. Once one examines the psychology of Elvis fans and how they relate to the Elvis legend, it's all too easy to be carried along by a kind of mythological drift. The legend begins to resemble an Arthurian saga, or the myths of the Fisher King that stretch clear back to the mists of prehistory. It follows a legend form that keeps occurring in the folktales of many cultures all over the world, folktales that are claimed by some academics to be the real basis for the story of Christ.

The Legend of the Boy King

The King is born in humble circumstances. No one suspects his true nature or real destiny apart from his doting and protective mother. As the King grows to manhood, key individuals begin to recognise his potential. He travels the country, as a singer of songs and a sexual shaman, attracting huge crowds to him. He rapidly gathers a vast following. Everywhere he goes, the young flock to his banner. As the King grows in strength and influence, the land enters a Golden Age. New Magic replaces the old, and new ways are replacing those that had gone before. The old rulers, however, fear and resent the power and the potency of this Boy King who has appeared out of nowhere to usurp the loyalties of the nation's youth. The Boy King is taken by soldiers. They insist that the time has come for him to cease his singing and shamanism. The law of the land demands that he became a warrior. In a public ritual, his hair is shorn, and under the guise of his becoming a warrior, he disappears into exile to a distant outpost of the Empire. The movement that he started continues, but it is leaderless and confused.

Eventually the King returns to the land, but this is not the Boy King of the Golden Age. He is remote and distant, constantly surrounded by courtiers, flatterers and sinister henchmen. His magic is diluted and seems to be fading. He never appears to his people in the flesh, and the only tangible proof that he continues to live at all are flickering images in dark places. The land falls upon evil times. Violence, revolution, and foreign war cast their shadows. Young and old are thrown against the other in angry conflict, but still the King doesn't return to his people, who now despair that he has permanently deserted them.

And then, when all seems lost, the King, at the symbolic age of thirty-three, invokes his power. His return is seen in every part of the land by the new magic. He is re-energised. For the first time in ten years, he comes among his people. Suddenly there is hope.

Again, though, the courtiers and flatterers surround the King. Isolated in his palace, he succumbs to solitary luxury. Lonely and alone, among servants and concubines, he dies. With his death, however, he transcends mere mortality, and miraculously, his power is returned to the people where it has always belonged. The people use his memory, his image, and his music to invoke that power. The King incarnate may be gone, but the King transcendental becomes immortal.

Yeah, I know what you're going to say. The writer has finally taken leave of his sanity. And yet, this is what you'd get if the story of Elvis had been handed down by an oral tradition rather than TV biographies and the works of Albert Goldman. Religions have been founded on a whole lot less. Could this be the secret of Elvis? That he was much more than just an entertainer, that he triggered something ancient and atavistic in some modern collective consciousness? Or have we just taken ourselves out to the ludicrous edge of fantasy? The Elvis Universe is one tricky cosmic neighbourhood.

I must have been about sixteen years old, going to one of the first all-night parties that I'd ever been to. I was in my first fledgling garage rock & roll band by this point. The guitar player was a kid with glasses who went by the name of Chub. His folks were wealthy, they had a big house, and most importantly, they were going to be away for the weekend. We'd all told our parents different stories to account for our being out all night, and early on Saturday evening, we converged on the home of Chub's family for what we devoutly hoped would be a feast of drunkenness and debauchery.

The truth was that we were too young and too callow for anything approaching true debauchery. We didn't know that debauchery takes years of practice. All we managed was to get beer drunk and stupid and ineptly paw at any of the girls present who were willing to let us. Around two in the morning, a lull ensued. Some of the kids had passed out, some were immobilized, some necking and groping. For some time, nobody had enough together to even put on a fresh record. After maybe fifteen minutes of listening to our own collective snoring, breathing, whispering, giggling and grunting, someone finally managed to collect themselves sufficiently to put on *Elvis*—Elvis' second album. Whoever did it may have been thinking more clearly than I imagined. Instead of dropping the stylus on the first track on side one, "Rip It Up," the record started with the plaintive moan of "Love Me."

"Treat me like a fool, treat me mean and cruel, but...love me."

I swear to God, after that first line, a sound came from every woman in that darkened room—from the floor and the depths of Chub's mother's couch, a swooning gasp, something between a sigh and a groan. It was as though they'd experienced a shock, somewhere out where pleasure meets the threshold of pain. At that moment, I realised beyond any shadow of a doubt that Elvis' voice did things to people.

Somebody once said, I forget who, that when things stop making sense, it's probably a good idea to start looking for magic. I've never had any real problem with the idea that a voice, Elvis at one extreme, maybe Adolf Hitler at the other, could act as a stimulant, perhaps even a narcotic, sidestepping rational perception, deductive logic, ducking under the speech centres and heading straight for the unconscious and the instinctive response. Perhaps there's another way to describe magic.

Some folks I talk to resist the idea, some react quite violently to this suggestion. I guess they have trouble accepting that they could be moved to involuntary acts by the Pavlovian command of a stranger, that magic could be worked on them and someone else could possess their will. Such loss of will is an anathema in this modern world that prides itself on both its ego and its logic, but the world has seen societies that have functioned quite adequately with the majority of their citizens indulging regularly and ritually in massive losses of ego and logic, and even entering trance states. The use of the voice has been a major part of many of these rituals. Chants, songs, monologs, call and response, anthems, psalms, and sermons are all part of the mystic menu to bring the individual to a heightened state and the group to a point of anything up to or including total mindless frenzy.

A glance at history also makes it virtually indisputable that certain individuals have quite definitely been able to sway their fellows by the power of their voices, and in some cases, actually change the course of history. Unfortunately, sound recording is a comparatively recent invention, and although we can read the words of an Abraham Lincoln, we have no idea of how his voice sounded. We don't know whether Napoleon had a quality of voice that inspired his men to march to Moscow. We have no idea how Alexander the Great persuaded an army of Greeks to follow him all the way to India. I've already mentioned Adolf Hitler. His voice was recorded and his image captured on film, and indeed, a couple of U.S. cable stations don't seem to be able to get through a single evening without running a show that features the sound and image of Hitler baying at his stormtroopers. These shows are designed to attract an audience of Americans who may not speak a single word of German, but who can tune in

HEAR IT

The FIRST collector's plate that plays "Blue Suede Shoes"

SEE IT

The FIRST collector's plate to capture the many faces of ELVIS in dramatic montage style art

FEEL IT

The FIRST collector's plate that makes you want to DANCE!

and experience a vicarious and hopefully guilty thrill of listening to a voice and watching the performance of the man who, in the twentieth century, had become the personification of evil.

What separates Elvis from Hitler, Napoleon, and Alexander the Great is that Elvis may have had a unique power in his voice, but he essentially had no verbal message. Elvis neither sang about freedom or exhorted anyone to conquer the world for him. Elvis operated on a subliteral level, and the response to him was also subliteral. Elvis sings, the women moan, the men wish that they were him, that they had the same power. Is it possible that something in the voice is pushing deep psychological buttons, and producing responses that, in some cases, are never forgotten. In interviews, fans describe a moment when they were "brought to Elvis." They can't define exactly what happened, but they know it happened. "I can't describe what it's like to fall in love, but I know when it's happening to me. That's how it was with Elvis."

❖　　　❖　　　❖

The final factor in the connection between Elvis and his fans/worshippers obviously has to be erotic. The young Elvis had a sexual charisma unlike anything that existed within the same time frame. The fifties were an era of unbelievable sexual repression, and Elvis bursted through the barriers with a uniquely joyous and crazy abandon. This is probably why my stepfather loathed him so much. He couldn't come to grips with the fact that my young male friends and I were being so intensely attracted to and influenced by such a potent male force. To his pre-rock & roll mindset, this could only indicate that there was something deeply wrong with us. Our attendant fixations with wearing our hair long and generally bucking the rules when we could only tended to confirm his worst fears. The truth was that what attracted us to Elvis wasn't any direct sexual connection, but the wild and heady freedom that he represented. We didn't want to fuck Elvis, we wanted to be Elvis. We wished we had his power to push the boundaries and break the chains, and we watched him intently, hoping that we could learn the secret.

Jim Morrison frequently declared that he was a Dionysian sexual shaman, and although Elvis has no such quasi-intellectual pretentions, the still photographs and few remaining film clips of the young Elvis' early stage shows

The women moan, the men wish they were him

reveal nothing less than, by the standards of the times, raucous communion of sexual chaos and disorder. Contemporary writers likened Elvis to a male stripper, and in so doing, clearly proved that they had totally missed the point. Elvis' bumps and grinds and blatant teasing may have had something in common with Tempest Storm and Lillie St. Cyr, but where the women strippers worked in an oppressive, rigidly controlled context as the audience sat silent, riveted, scarcely daring to move a muscle, let alone give vent to a reaction, Elvis exploded the bomb and turned a club or concert hall into a screaming explosion of unleashed emotions. As Elvis himself put it—"Singing rhythm and blues really knocks it out. I watch my audiences and I listen to them and I know we're all getting something out of our system but none of us knows what it is. The important thing is that we're getting rid of it and nobody's getting hurt."

Rudolph Paulini, Munich 1959

**Elvis boasted that he had slept
with over a thousand women**

Even though it is clearly one of the central dynamics in the relationship between Elvis and his followers, sex occupies a somewhat uneasy position in the Elvis Universe. Many of the most devoted followers exhibit what can only be described as a definite prudery in their relationship to Elvis. They seem much more comfortable with the later, formalised, Las Vegas rituals of handing out silk scarves than the orgiastic scrimmages that were the early Elvis shows. Many of the fans I've talked to over the years seem to treat Elvis like some kind of guilty pleasure, and quickly back away from the idea that they might have gone to bed with Elvis Presley if the chance had ever presented itself. A similar uneasiness manifests itself when the subject of Elvis' sex life comes up.

Elvis, even by his own admission, was a highly sexual individual. On more than one occasion, he boasted that he had slept with well over a thousand women. Canadian rocker Ronnie Hawkins summed up the general perception of Elvis' sexual prowess in the standard speech he made to new recruits for his back-up band—"The pay ain't much, but you'll get more pussy than Elvis." Dennis Hopper recounts how, during Elvis' first stay in Hollywood, he'd hole up in his hotel suite for days on end while a seemingly endless stream of women passed through his bedroom. And yet, a large number of fans seem to go into virtual denial when these aspects of Elvis are so much as mentioned. I clearly recall at the Memphis premier of the documentary film *This Is Elvis,* a gasp of shock when, during the course of the movie, Elvis, leaving a show in the back of a limo, talks ribaldly about a women he was with the previous night. This was not the kind of thing the loyal fans wanted to know about, let alone hear about from Elvis himself.

It would almost seem as though one section of Elvis fans have, somewhere along the line, exchanged the roll & roll sexual ecstasy for something closer to a religious fervour, and it would seem that, when the fervour turns religious, the object of that fervour is expected to be an immaculate and Christ-like individual. This becomes even more understandable when one remembers that a large proportion of the hardest of hard-core Elvis fans—particularly those from the South—come from a blue collar, fundamentalist background and may have, quite literally, traded Jesus for Elvis.

Some have even attempted to solve the dilemma of how to reconcile Elvis the sacred and Elvis the profane by coming up with the deeply weird theory that Elvis was in fact two people in one: the original Elvis spirit and the spirit of Jesse Garon, the twin who died at birth. These two entities are in constant conflict for domination of the single body. Elvis is all that's good, pure, and spiritual, while Jesse Garon is the Dark Side of the Force, black leather on the halfshell, hell bent on chaos and outrage, sex, drugs, and rock & roll. Elvis loved his mother and Jesse Garon killed televisions.

The fact that Elvis theorising is already able to go through such alarming metaphysical contortion would appear to be yet another pointer in the direction of the highly confusing conclusion that the worship of Elvis Presley is taking on a lot of the attributes of an actual religion.

❖   ❖   ❖

Just to confuse matters further, since the early eighties, a third Elvis has started to emerge. For some perverse reason, almost certainly connected with the overkill of excess that became Elvis' lifestyle in the years just prior to his death, punk rockers and those who came after them have remained fascinated by Elvis. The Clash mimicked the cover of Elvis' first LP for the sleeve design of their album *London Calling.* The Smiths went one better and featured a high school photo of Elvis with a bow tie and a bad case of acne on the sleeve of one of their 12" singles. A 1981 compilation album of Southern Californian punk bands was titled *The Future Looks Bright Ahead* and the cover art shows a horrified Elvis staring into a crystal ball.

For the punks, Elvis provided the ultimate confirmation of the nihilist message that contemporary society offers no future and even the most unbelievable success will ultimately decay into downfall, degradation and death. Punk's constant use of Elvis as a symbol, as a bizarre icon, or some huge rock & roll object lesson, has actually opened up a whole new quadrant in the Elvis Universe.

The Third Elvis is very obviously absurd. He's the Elvis that dwells in

Elvis – The Next Generation

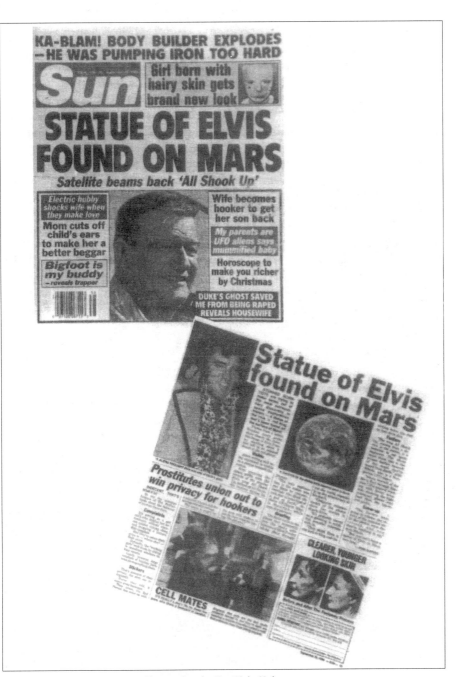

Expansion in the Elvis Universe

tabloid fantasies. He's the Elvis who has statues erected to him on the planet Mars. He's the Elvis who rides in flying saucers and communes with aliens. He's the Elvis who haunts the pool house at Graceland. He's the Elvis who sends spirit messages to Wayne Newton. The Third Elvis was the one played by John Belushi and Eddie Murphy on "Saturday Night Live," and blew the lines of "That's When Your Heartaches Begin" live on stage. Just as this book was going to press, the news broke that the Third Elvis' daughter had married Michael Jackson. The Third Elvis is enormously fat, clad in polyester, is continuously eating, needs sixteen Quaaludes to get a good night's sleep, visits with Richard Nixon at the White House, and always carries a gun, always strapped and ready to shoot out the TV set or the Ferrari.

Although the Third Elvis initially seems to be a figure viewed from a perspective of relentless cruelty, the fact that he shows no signs of either fading or going away would appear to indicate that the mockery that is his lot must be tempered with a certain degree of twisted affection. Even the outrageous punk rumour that Elvis' body was switched after his death with an anonymous corpse, and the real body was ground down to hamburger to be eaten in cannibal rituals by contemporary rock mega-stars, says more about the punks' opinion of Mick Jagger and his ilk than about Elvis himself.

Through the eighties and nineties, the Quadrant of the Third Elvis even began to solidify and take on a tangible shape. Through the paintings of Joni Mabe, the songs of Nick Cave, and bands like Tijuana Bible, it has developed a form and a structure. To be sure, it's a dark and sinister place, the final stop of the black mystery train with its sixteen coaches, a mythic view of the deep South, filled with alligator swamps and haunted, brooding, ante-bellum mansions, with dark, ancient oaks, heavy with Spanish moss, and heat lightning crackling at the horizon. It's the same world where Jimi Hendrix choked on his own vomit, Robert Johnson went to the crossroads at midnight to sell his soul to the Devil, and Blind Lemon Jefferson's only request was to see that his grave was kept clean.

The irony is that, despite the obvious irreverence, and being as about as diametrically opposed to the fans of the second Vegas Elvis as is possible, the Third Elvis, in its own way, is another attempt to put a mystic spin on the continuing fascination with Elvis Presley.

And there we have it. When I first sat down to write this introduction, I was well aware that there would be no simple answer to the puzzle of why devotion to Elvis continues to grow and flourish. We have touched most of the obvious bases and probably the only thing that's made itself clear is that Elvis refuses to leave the culture, that the mythology is now rapidly starting to obscure both the man and the artist. Elvis worship really does seem to be approaching a collective state-of-mind that, if not an actual quasi-religion, represents something that is pretty damn close to it.

Sex, rock & roll, youth rebellion, some innate quality of Elvis' voice, television, magic, a unique convergence of time and place may have all played a part in the impact that Elvis Presley had on Western culture during the second half of the twentieth century. None of these factors on their own, however, provide an entire answer, and even combined together, they still come up short. Perhaps we have to look beyond the rational and the logical for the answers to the paradoxes that surround the memory of Elvis, and perhaps that's why I needed to invent a comic book Elvis Universe and why others take refuge in myth and legend, the mystic and the metaphysical.

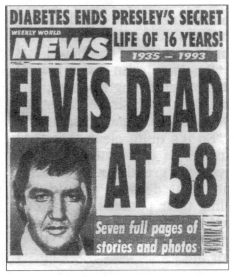

About the only thing I know for sure is that Elvis and the Elvis Universe continues. Elvis abides. As I finish writing this, the world has its ass in uproar about Lisa Marie Presley's marriage to Michael Jackson. A couple of days ago someone asked me what I thought that was all about. The only answer I could give was perhaps she'd married Michael because he was the first man she'd met since her father who'd been anywhere near as close to—and who had seen anything like as clearly—the true madness of humanity when they choose an idol. Meanwhile, on the seventeenth anniversary of her father's death, I watch the line of pilgrims carrying their candles through the gardens of Graceland. I know something's happening, but I wonder if I'll ever know what it is.

—Mick Farren, 16 August 1994.

Elvis and Debra Paget

When I first started out on this project, the idea was to produce a simple catalogue of Elvis merchandise. Since that time, matters have radically changed. The first things that I discovered was that there's actually enough Elvis merchandise, both ancient and modern, official and unofficial, to fill several volumes and keep a team of writers and researchers busy for a couple of years or more cataloging it. Beyond that, I also found that there were a bunch of books, good, bad, and mind-boggling, that listed and even set prices for most of the Elvis memorabilia, merchandise, junk, and just plain stuff that's around today.

My second major discovery was that, while researching the original concept, I started to unearth long lists of far more interesting facts, factoids, rumours, gossip, and trivia. Thus, rather than bore you with yet another volume full of Elvis sugar shakers, silk scarves, and license plate holders, I have created one mighty alphabetised list of as many of the people, places and inanimate objects that create the shape of what I quickly started to think of as the Elvis Universe. The further I went, the more fun it became. The lists started to include Elvis' more prominent lovers, and the women who had claimed he'd fathered their children. I started listing the more outrageous stories from the supermarket tabloids. I began, item by item, to get vectors on Elvis' own conspicuous consumption, and from that, the near-madness of the life that Elvis the man was forced to lead. As I waded through the conspiracy theories, the weird beliefs, the prime impersonators and the extremist fans, I got another handle on the external hysteria that constantly surrounded and imprisoned him and still continues to this day.

I can neither claim that this little book is complete or the final word. The project became more and more complicated and time-consuming, and I can only be grateful that the publishers had an almost infinite measure of patience while I was working it out. At a certain point, I had to take a deep breath and declare that enough was enough. That's what you have here. Make of it what you will. You may flip through it and find a bunch of amusing and bizarre products, people, and trivia. Another alternative is that you can plough through the whole thing from A–Z, and then you may start to see some traces of the same shape that I began to perceive in the strange phenomena that we have made of Elvis Presley. Or maybe not. Just as Elvis can be all things to all people, no two people have the same perspective on Elvis. All I can really say is that I'm showing you mine. Maybe one day, you'll be in a position to show me yours.

Back when I started to write this book, I mailed off an order for an Elvis TCB (Taking Care of Business) pendant, a reproduction of the one that Elvis handed out to his staff, flunkies, retainers, and henchmen. Months later, after a number of phone calls and a series of truly strange glitches and foul-ups, the pendant was delivered. It actually arrived by UPS yesterday. Yesterday was August 16, the anniversary of Elvis' death. The TV stations are all running Elvis movies and newscasts from Graceland. Today, I finally finished the book. That's what Carl Jung called synchronicity, and it kinda makes you think....

The Hitchhiker's Guide To Elvis

Aaron/Aron

A certain confusion has always surrounded the correct spelling of Elvis Presley's middle name. On his birth certificate (filled out by Vernon Presley, his father), it was spelled "Aron." On his gravestone, however, it is plainly spelled "Aaron." For Elvis' name to be misspelled on his own tomb would seem to be too much for even a down-home, Tennessee screw-up. The truth is that the mistake was made on the birth certificate, an error that Elvis corrected later in life when he legally formalised his full name as "Elvis Aaron Presley."

This correction, though, didn't apparently make it through to RCA Records, who, as late as 1980, released an album titled *Elvis Aron Presley*.

Some of the more paranoid fans attempted to weave the spelling confusion into the ongoing Elvis conspiracy theories, speculating that the spelling on headstone was a secret message indicating the body in the grave at Graceland was not that of Elvis.

Adams, Nick

During Elvis' early days in Hollywood, through the time that he was making *Love Me Tender*, he was befriended by some of the people who had previously constituted the entourage of the late James Dean. Elvis even dated Natalie Wood for a while. Among the ex-Dean crowd was actor Nick Adams, who would later play Johnny Yuma in the TV western series, "The Rebel."

These new-found Hollywood friends scared the hell out of Colonel Tom Parker, who feared they might weaken his control over Elvis. Accordingly, the Colonel placed Adams on a secret cash retainer to act as a spy in the Elvis camp and report back to the Colonel as to whom Elvis might be talking and the subject of their conversations.

Nick Adams died of an overdose of paraldehyde and tranquilizers in 1968. *(see also JAMES DEAN STORY, THE and WOOD, NATALIE.)*

Address book

A number of Elvis address books can be found in stationery stores and novelty shops. The official Graceland address book has a colour picture of Elvis in his famous gold lame suit under a clear acrylic cover that bears the inscription, "The Sun Never Sets On A Legend." *(see also GOLD SUIT.)*

Afghan

An Elvis Presley Afghan of 100% cotton which can be used as a throw rug or wall hanging shows a picture of the Vegas-era Elvis and comes in blue, green, rose, or cranberry, and by the standards of Elvis collectibles, is actually quite nicely designed.

Available from Graceland Gifts, 3734 Elvis Presley Boulevard, Memphis, TN 38116.

Alan (code name)

Private code name.

When Ursula Andress (among others) wanted to speak directly to Elvis at Graceland, she was instructed to use ask for Elvis using the code name "Alan."

Alan (imitator)

Elvis imitator *(see MEYER, ALAN.)*

Alden, Ginger

Memphis' "Miss Traffic Safety of 1976" was Elvis' last girlfriend. Initially, Elvis had been hot for her sister Terry Alden, the 1976 "Miss Tennessee," but when a date was arranged by DJ George Klein, Ginger tagged along and succeeded in snagging Elvis herself. She subsequently took up residence in Graceland and was the person who first discovered Elvis' body after his death.

Ms. Alden would benefit materially from her relationship with Elvis. While he was alive, he lavished gifts on her including a $12,000 white Lincoln Continental Mark V and a $70,000 diamond ring. After his death, Ginger made a number of efforts to cash in on her role in the drama as the woman who was with him when he died. Her claim that Elvis had proposed to her, and that they were to be married on Christmas Day 1977 in a Greek Orthodox Ceremony has never been satisfactorily confirmed, though.

In September 1977, she sold the story of her last day with Elvis to the *National Enquirer.* Seven months later, in a second *Enquirer* story, she claimed that she was in psychic dream contact with Elvis, and that her mother, Jo Laverne, had seen Elvis' ghost. In 1980, she cut a record—*I'd Rather Have A Memory Than A Dream*, and in the same year, appeared in a low budget, fictionalized bio-pic titled *The Living Legend.* Ginger Alden continues to act in TV commercials.

Ghostly contacts notwithstanding, Jo Laverne Alden sued the estate of Elvis Presley in 1978 for $40,000, claiming that Elvis had promised to pay off her home mortgage and divorce costs. The suit was dismissed. *(see also SIGHTINGS.)*

UFO alien sang 'Love Me Tender'

● **UFO alien like above serenaded scared farmer**

HIS HEART pounding in fear as he watched a huge glowing object descend from the sky, a farmer breathed a heartfelt sigh of relief when he heard a strange visitor from outer space serenade him with a favorite tune that would have sent the King of Rock 'n' Roll reeling in his grave.

Gifford Marvinson says he was terrified of the flying object that landed in his front yard until he was greeted by a strange space alien singing *Love Me Tender*, the song made famous by Elvis Presley.

Elvis fan

"I thought I was going to be zapped with a death-ray gun or kidnapped for heinous experiments until I heard the creature singing to me," explains Gifford, 45.

"A calm suddenly fell over me and I felt at one with the entire universe. The alien was singing the song like the King himself," adds the farmer, who has been an Elvis fan most of his life.

Gifford had been sitting in the living room watching a late-night television show while his wife and two children slept when he noticed a bright

STORY by FRED SLEEVES

light outside the window.

"I went outside and saw a giant, bright yellow object coming closer and closer to the ground. It made only a humming sound, and it landed in my front yard. It was as big as the house.

"I was frozen with fear as I watched a huge door open in front and then a small creature emerge. I thought it was going to kill me. It was about 4 feet tall with a yellow glow surrounding it.

"Then the alien started singing. The words were coming out with a strange synthesizer-like sound."

Too stunned

After the song was over, the alien bowed and stared at Gifford for a few moments before going back into the ship, which lifted off and was gone in seconds from his farm north of Birmingham, England.

"I guess it was some form of greeting, to show they meant no harm," says Gifford. "But I was too stunned to respond."

...claims farmer

Gifford's two children report waking up to see a huge light out their window when the object was taking off. His wife Marian says she heard the song.

"I was in bed, too tired to get up, and thought Gifford was playing records," she says.

Drinking man

"I recognized the song, but it did sound much different than before. It was strange. I believe Gifford saw what he says he saw. My husband's not a drinking man, as some skeptics are saying."

Gifford theorizes the aliens picked up the sounds of his records, and since he often plays Elvis tunes, they attempted to communicate with the tender love ballad.

— *FRED SLEEVES*

odds...

A DOZEN SILVER foil packets are nestled in a red heart-decorated box. The product is a real hot item in today's marketplace — sweet Condom-Mints.

Aliens

Since Elvis' death in 1977, and particularly during the furor over the idea that Elvis was still alive—when people seemed to be spotting him in the most unlikely places, almost in the manner of Bigfoot—a number of the supermarket tabloids attempted to link Elvis with their other standard and standby subjects, Unidentified Flying Objects and extraterrestrial visitors. One typical story appeared in the *Sun* on 9 February 1988:

"His heart pounded in fear as he watched the huge glowing object descend from the sky, a farmer breathed a sigh of relief when he heard a strange visitor from outer space serenade him with a favorite tune that would have sent the King of Rock 'n' Roll spinning in his grave.

"Gifford Marvinson says he was terrified of the flying object that landed in his front yard until he was greeted by a strange space alien singing 'Love Me Tender,' the song made famous by Elvis Presley."

Other stories reported Elvis having been seen peering from the porthole of a UFO, and Elvis artifacts being discovered on the Moon and Mars. *(see also FACE ON MARS, THE; SIGHTINGS; and UFOS.)*

All-American Boy

Sometime around 1958, a character called Bill Parsons (in fact, country star Bobby Bare recording under a phony name) put out a record on the Fraternity label. The title was "All American Boy," and although little more than a crassly traditional "talking blues," it basically said it all in respect to the dreams that Elvis had opened up for every kid with a cheap guitar who believed that he could grow sideburns. Some of those kids were John Lennon and Bob Dylan. Others weren't. The first lines were:

> You get a guitar and you put it in tune,
> And you'll be rockin' and rollin' soon.
> Ridin' around in a Cadillac,
> Fightin' the girls offa your back.

Anagram

Fan Theory circa 1989.

During the "Elvis is alive" furor of the late eighties, the fact that one anagram of the word Elvis is "lives" was fixed on by some fans as corroborative evidence that Elvis was alive.

A second anagram worth noting appears during the credits of the Robert Redford movie *Sneakers*. Rearrange the letters of "Universal Pictures" and you get the message "A turnip cures Elvis."

Ann-Margret

In the Elvis Universe and the minds of all but a handful of Elvis fans, Ann-Margret was the Queen Who Never Was. For a while there, back in the sixties, particularly in the wake of *Viva Las Vegas*, it seemed as though the unbelievable might happen and Elvis and Ann-Margret would marry and found the dream dynasty. At one point, Ann-Margret actually went public with an announcement of an impending engagement, although the Parker office moved quickly to contradict the story.

That Elvis and Ann-Margret should be husband and wife made such perfect fan magazine sense, him with his dark, good looks, her with flaming red hair, and as Little Richard put it "a body built to please." In idle moments, one might imagine them having sex together, and it just seemed so right. They even seemed to work well together professionally. Ann-Margret brought a whole new level of individual energy to *Viva Las Vegas* that seemed to elevate it to a higher level than so many of the other fun-in-the-sun Elvis musicals.

Of course, it was never to be. Even in her autobiography, Ann-Margret seems reluctant to talk about what really went down between her and Elvis. Maybe he really did prefer Priscilla. Maybe he wouldn't give up his lifestyle and

Elvis and Ann-Margret

other women. Or maybe Ann-Margret realised, like Natalie Wood before her, and like Priscilla years later, the reality of being Elvis' wife was just about as impossible and destructive as being Elvis. We can speculate all we want, but sadly it will make us none the wiser. Like so many of the dreams in the Elvis universe, it was never to be.

When Ann-Margret called Elvis at Graceland, she used the code name "Thumper," after the rabbit in *Bambi. (see also WOOD, NATALIE.)*

Apollo Theater

Elvis never appeared at the Apollo, the theatre that had been the Mecca for black performers for more than half a century. Buddy Holly was the first white rocker to play there. However, on Elvis' first visit to New York in 1955, after auditioning for Arthur Godfrey's Talent Scouts, he made the pilgrimage up to Harlem to see R&B legend Bo Diddley and hang out backstage. *(see also GOD-FREY, ARTHUR.)*

Apostolakos, Kiki

Kiki Apostolakos is a well known figure to the staff at Graceland, and she can frequently be seen standing in thoughtful silence in the Meditation Gardens, beside Elvis' grave, just after dawn before the tourists start arriving. Kiki Apostolakos can't be described as typical of the extreme Elvis fan, because at those extremes, no real norms exist and there are no real types. All the extreme Elvis fans really have in common is the willingness to place their devotion to Elvis above the demands of their own lives and their own happiness. In this, they are indistinguishable from the fanatical followers of some strange and demanding cult.

Kiki Apostolakos would not have even described herself as a moderate Elvis fan before his death. It was only when he died that she was hit by an emotional response that left her quite literally stunned. "I was like a robot. I had no appetite for anything. I kept asking myself, why am I living?"

Ultimately she would leave her family in Greece, including her two daughters, and through a marriage of convenience emigrate to the U.S.A., to Memphis, where, except for the time she spends working as a waitress to support herself, she devotes all of her life to the memory of Elvis. To say that the extreme fringes of Elvis fandom are composed of the desperate and the dysfunctional might be an exaggeration, but they certainly have much more than their fair share of crazies, something else in which Elvis worship resembles a religious cult.

Are You Hungry Tonight?

Hardback book, 1992. By Brenda Arlene Butler: Gramercy Books.

This slim volume is one of a number of Elvis-inspired cookbooks that came on the market in the late eighties and early nineties. Lavishly illustrated and dangerously heavy on the cholesterol, it contains instructions for preparing some sixty-five dishes that it claims were among Elvis' favourites. It also has the construction specifications for the giant wedding cake that was provided for Elvis' 1967 wedding to Priscilla.

Available from bookstores.

Are You Lonesome Tonight?

Hardback book, 1987. By Lucy de Barbin and Dary Matera: Villiard Books.

Lucy de Barbin charges/confesses that, following a 1953 affair with the eighteen-year-old Elvis, she bore his illegitimate daughter (named Desiree, after the movie of the same name in which Marlon Brando played Napoleon). This caused a considerable media furor when this book appeared in 1987, accompanied by a massive promotional campaign.

De Barbin cited tapes and a written poem that Elvis had given her as support for her claims. The handwriting of the poem was analyzed and judged genuine by Charles Hamilton, the expert who, in 1983, blew the whistle on the phony Clifford Irving's "Hitler Diaries." The tapes were never subjected to expert technical scrutiny.

At the same time, the Memphis Mafia, headed by Joe Esposito, closed ranks against Ms. de Barbin, declaring that the liaison between her and Elvis couldn't have run the prolonged course described in her book without them getting wind of it, and that they knew nothing. Geraldo Rivera investigated the de Barbin story for the TV show "Entertainment Tonight," but failed to be convinced. *(see also MEMPHIS MAFIA, THE and RIVERA, GERALDO.)*

Can still be still be found in bookstores.

Art Can

Novelty item, 1994.

This has to be one of the weirdest Elvis items ever marketed. To all outward appearances, the "art can" is the same as a standard twelve-ounce soda or beer can, except that it contains a small, battery-powered motor that causes it to rock and vibrate when turned on. The can bears a painting of the young Elvis live on stage and the words "All Shook Up" and "Elvis" on a purple background.

Available from Graceland Gifts, 1-800-238-2000.

Atlantic Records

In 1955, when it was clear that Elvis' career was taking off too fast for him to remain on Sam Phillips' Sun label, Ahmed Ertegun, the president of Atlantic Records—back then a primarily black, R&B label—offered Colonel Tom Parker $25,000 to sign Elvis.

Unfortunately for Atlantic, RCA almost doubled the offer with a bid of $45,000, which the Colonel accepted, and the rest is history. We can only guess what direction Elvis' work might have taken under the direction of Ertegun, the man who made stars out of Ben E. King, Ray Charles, and Aretha Franklin.

Atomic Powered Singer, The

This is how Elvis was billed on his April 1956 debut at the New Frontier Hotel in Las Vegas.

Baseball caps

The baseball cap has now become such a standard item that at least twenty or more varieties of Elvis baseball caps, both officially sanctioned or otherwise, are available at souvenir, novelty, and clothing stores. A recent addition, a black baseball cap bearing the TCB lightning flash logo, makes the wearer look a little like some kind of neo-stormtrooper. *(see also TCB.)*

Baseball jackets

Just like the baseball caps, Elvis-related silk or nylon baseball style warm-up jackets are available in a variety of styles and designs.

Baxter, Sir Malcolm

The *Weekly World News* of 22 April 1980 revealed that, according to Dr. Barbara Williams and Dr. Carl Giles, Elvis had been reincarnated on this planet no less than four previous times. The most recent incarnation was in the form of an eighteenth century English aristocrat, Sir Malcolm Baxter, from the county of Sussex in southeast England. Elvis/Malcolm apparently also suffered from drug problems in this life, presumably with opium, about the only narcotic available in England in the eighteenth century. Other previous incarnations included a citizen of ancient Greece, an inhabitant of Atlantis, and an Irish sheep farmer. *(see also SIGHTINGS.)*

Beatles, The

The Beatles were all powerful admirers of Elvis Presley, particularly John Lennon, who bordered on being an Elvis obsessive. In the band's early days in Hamburg, when performances were particularly rough and ready, it was said that Lennon would drop into Elvis imitations any time that he was given half the chance.

The legendary meeting between Elvis and the Beatles occurred during the Beatles second tour of the U.S. It took place on 27 August 1965 (a Friday night); John, Paul, George, and Ringo arrived at Elvis' Bel Air home (565 Peruguia

8/27/65 — THE BEATLES AT ELVIS' BEL AIR HOUSE.

Way) at around 10 P.M. and stayed until two the following morning. The Beatles drank scotch while Elvis stuck to 7-Up, and at some point during the evening, they jammed together in Elvis' music room. The persistent legend was that tapes existed of the jam, although this was denied by George Harrison in a 1987 interview in *Creem*. Fans live in hope, however, that one day an Elvis-meets-the-Beatles tape will be bootlegged out or otherwise revealed unto us. It has however been thirty years now and we're still waiting.

In the immediate aftermath of the meeting, the Beatles were full of praise for Elvis—"fab," "gear," "just like one of us"—later, however, opinions were modified. When asked to describe Elvis, Ringo's only comment was "strange." Likewise with Elvis, who dissed the group as Commie subversives when he was looking to grease his way in with Richard Nixon. *(see also NIXON, RICHARD MILHOUSE.)*

Behind Closed Doors

Hardback book, 1994. By Paul Lichter.

A photo collection of Elvis at home and with his family with "touching accounts by Paul Lichter." Okay? *(see also LICHTER, PAUL.)*

Available in bookstores.

Bel Air Club

Memphis landmark, 1850 S. Bellvue Boulevard.

The Bel Air Club which was part of the Bel Air Motel was one of Elvis' earliest gigs. Through 1954, he did guest spots with both Doug Poindexter and his Starlight Wranglers and the Jack Clement band.

Beaulieu, Priscilla Ann

(see PRESLEY, PRISCILLA.)

Best of Elvis, The

Trade paperback book, 1994. By Cindy Hazen and Mike Freeman.

A collection of the wit and wisdom of Elvis, subtitled "recollections of a great humanitarian."

Available in bookstores.

Bible

A Bible belonging to Elvis (he claimed to have a Bible in every room of his home) was sold at an auction in Memphis for $1,375.

Black, Bill

Bill Black was born William P. Black in Memphis in 1926 and played stand-up bass behind Elvis through the crucial make-or-break period of 1955–7. After being dropped by Elvis in 1957, Black went on to record with the Bill Black Combo and have hits with "Smokie Part 2" (Hi 2018) and "White Silver Sands" (Hi 2021). Bill Black died of a brain tumour in October 1965. The bass that Bill Black used when he backed Elvis is currently owned by Paul McCartney. *(see also BLUE MOON BOYS; ELVIS – TV SERIES; and MOORE, SCOTTY.)*

Black Leather Suit

Elvis had a gut instinct that black and pink were the colours of rock & roll. Of course, Elvis' major problem was that he all too often allowed himself to be diverted from his gut instinct, as evidenced by the snappy casuals that passed as costume in the bulk of his movies, or the white or baby blue, bell-bottomed jumpsuits-of-lights that he wore for his seventies stage shows.

When, however, Elvis was fighting for his career on his 1968 NBC TV special, his gut instinct managed to assert itself and take control, and he performed the hard rock segment of the show in a black leather suit, much in the manner of Gene Vincent or Jim Morrison.

A life-size, full colour, free-standing cardboard cutout of Elvis in a black leather suit can be found a many of the hipper novelty stores. It is not, however, the suit from the TV special, but a more elaborate one with fringes.

Blue Moon Boys

This was the collective title used through 1955 by Bill Black and Scotty Moore, Elvis' first and arguably greatest back-up band. When, in September of 1957, Scotty and Bill demanded a pay hike—the duo were still only making a couple

Black Leather Suit

of hundred bucks a week while Elvis was amassing millions—the Colonel dropped them from the payroll and Elvis made no major objection. Despite the crucial part that these two musicians played in the creation of Elvis' original sound, they would never be permanently rehired.

A somewhat romanticised version of Elvis, Scotty, and Bill's adventures on the road in the early Sun Records days was the core of the 1990 TV series "Elvis." *(see also BLACK, BILL; MOORE, SCOTTY; and ELVIS – TV SERIES.)*

Reproductions of an original playbill style poster—printed from the original type—for Elvis and the Blue Moon Boys at the Florida Theatre in Jacksonville were marketed in the mid-eighties by Hatch Show Print of Nashville, Tenn. Unfortunately, Hatch Show Print is now out of business, but copies of the posters still show up in specialist rock collector stores.

Books

Under U.S. law, all products bearing the likeness and name of Elvis Presley have to be licensed or otherwise authorized by Elvis Presley Enterprises. The only exception is books. Because of the free speech provisions of the United States Constitution, any damned fool can write a book about Elvis any time he feels like it, and any damned fool can publish it. That's what's known as freedom of expression.

Boone, Pat

The anti-Elvis.

Brewer-Giorgio, Gayle

Gayle Brewer-Giorgio is the author of the novel *Orion* and the non-fiction book *Is Elvis Alive?* Her seemingly unshakable theory that Elvis is still living somewhere in seclusion has made her the leading figure in what can only be called the Elvis conspiracy business. With three books and two syndicated TV specials on the subject to her credit, Ms. Brewer-Giorgio has done very well with the conspiracy business. *(see also IS ELVIS ALIVE? and ORION.)*

Bubble gum

Novelty candy, 1957 and 1978.

Elvis Presley bubble gum was marketed on two separate occasions, once in the fifties and once just after Elvis' death. Both times it came with baseball-style trading cards and was manufactured under license from Colonel Tom Parker.

The gum was terrible.

The fifties trading cards are now only obtainable as collectors items in rock

memorabilia, and specialist trading card stores. The seventies gum was manufactured by Donruss Inc., Memphis, Tenn. 38101, and can now and again be
found in candy stores.

Burke's Florist

Memphis landmark at 1609 Elvis Presley Boulevard.

The store where all the flowers for Graceland were purchased, including
those supplied for Elvis' funeral.

Burrows, Jon

A Weekend World Plus "photograph"
claiming to be of Elvis as he is now

One of the stories that circulated in the late
eighties, along with all the other claims that
Elvis had faked his own death, was that he
was living under the alias Jon Burrows
either in Hawaii or (of all places)
Kalamazoo, Michigan (as it turns out,
Kalamazoo is also reputed to be a notorious
UFO hotspot with flying saucer sightings
reported on an almost daily basis.) The
weekly supermarket tabloids were also
quick to latch on to the concept of Elvis at
large, and the *Weekly World News* even
went so far as to produce a composite portrait of a bearded, aging Elvis as an aid to
recognising the King should any of their
readers happen across him at Wendy's or in

the checkout line at the supermarket. *(see also IS ELVIS ALIVE? and SIGHT-INGS.)*

Busts

I have yet to come across a bronze bust of Elvis in the classic tradition, but I fully expect that one will appear in the near future. Ceramic busts, on the other hand, have been available in modest profusion for at least the last ten years. The most readily available busts of Elvis come in two distinct designs. By far the most popular is the life-size, early Vegas model in Plaster of Paris. The head—with hair in the style of Michelangelo's *David*—is framed by a typical Elvis stand-up regency collar and a loose scarf draped around the neck. The majority of examples are hand painted in supposedly authentic colours: black hair, pink skin, and a white jump suit collar with blue spangles. The scarf is usually also blue, but I have seen less common examples in which it is blue and yellow. Other variations include unpainted versions in plain white and ones sprayed matte black to resemble a bronze cast. Individual artists have also customised individual busts to create everything from dayglo alien Elvises to Elvis in warpaint. Some busts come wired to take an electric light and shade.

The second common type is smaller, about six inches from chin to hairline, and from the way the features are modeled, almost certainly originates in India or Pakistan. This is a simple head and neck type of bust, so no clothing is portrayed, but from the haircut and general look of the works, it seems to be modeled on the sixties Elvis of the Hollywood movie years. The "Indian" bust is a good deal harder to find than the larger versions and is more standardized in its colouring and finish. The skin tones are a little darker than are strictly natural, another indication of its of origin.

These Elvis busts are perfect examples of the kind of "underground" Elvis marketing that exists with very little organized distribution and certainly no authorization or approval from Graceland, Elvis Presley Enterprises, or the Elvis Presley Estate. Even the exact origins of these items are far from clear. I once stumbled upon a warehouse in Tijuana, Mexico, that was full of raw plaster Elvis busts (the larger, more common model) lined up, waiting to be painted, but I very much doubt that this was the only place in the world where they're manufactured. On this level, all you need is the mold, the plaster, and a lot of cheap labour to paint the suckers, and you're in the Elvis business. And as much as this sort of illicit enterprise may irk them, there's nothing that the Presley estate can really do about it.

The Elvis busts could originally be found on sale as ornaments in discount furniture stores along with the plaster tigers, ceramic dogs, and bad art-deco knock-offs. Today, though, they regularly find their way into the hip novelty stores in most major cities. *(see also INDIA.)*

Buttons

The number of buttons and lapel badges that carry the likeness of Elvis now runs into the hundreds, if not the thousands. An optical badge from the fifties that still shows up in collectors' stores features Elvis in two different poses when looked at from different angles. When moved quickly, it produces the illusion of Elvis performing. A very nice enamel pin that shows flames and the words "Burning Love" is currently on sale in gift stores in Las Vegas.

Cadillac

Elvis and Cadillacs were almost synonymous. He owned them, he gave them away, and he was carried to his grave in one. His major ambition while he was struggling to make it was to own a big shiny Cadillac. His first purchase after the money started rolling in was a customised pink convertible for his mother, and a more serviceable four-door Fleetwood for himself and the band, the one that according to legend, "caught fire and burned up on the road." *(see also TRUTH ABOUT ME, THE.)*

> You may go to college,
> You may go to school,
> You may drive a pink Cadillac,
> But don't you be nobody's fool.
> > ("Baby Let's Play House" by Arthur Gunter.
> > Recorded by Elvis in 1955.)

> Got no sleigh with reindeer,
> No sack on my back,
> You gonna see me coming,
> In a big black Cadillac.
> > ("Santa Claus Is Back In Town" by Jerry
> > Leiber and Mike Stoller. Recorded by Elvis
> > in 1957.)

Cake

When Elvis married Priscilla Beaulieu at the Aladdin Casino in Las Vegas on 1 May 1967, the five-tier pink and white wedding cake decorated with hearts, silver bells, and red roses was over seven feet high and contained, among other ingredients, a total of fifty-eight pounds of sugar and nineteen pounds of Crisco.

Candles

From the late eighties onwards, "sacred" Elvis candles started appearing in stores alongside the more regular novena candles that carried images of Jesus, The Virgin Mary, St. Michael, and St. John the Conqueror.

Captain Marvel, Jr.

Captain Marvel, Jr., the Most Powerful Boy in the World, who appeared in Fawcett Publications *Master Comics* in the 1940s, was Elvis' boyhood comic book hero, seemingly almost to the point of juvenile obsession. Certainly Elvis seemed to base his teenage, pre-fame hairstyle on the character. Unlike Robin or Bucky Barnes, the boy sidekicks of Batman and Captain America, who were totally subservient to their adult mentors, or Superboy, who was merely Superman at an earlier age, Captain Marvel, Jr. was created by Captain Marvel, but after that, he functioned independently in his own comic book and along his own separate story lines.

The origin of Captain Marvel, Jr. is a strange one, even by comic book superhero standards. Captain Marvel (Sr.) is doing battle with Hitler's super-hero creation Captain Nazi, and manages to hurl the arch-villain from a moving airplane. Captain Nazi plunges into the waters of a bay, where he is rescued by an old man and his grandson who are fishing in a boat. Being the embodiment of evil, Captain Nazi repays their kindness by killing the grandfather and maiming the boy. Captain Marvel rescues the boy, whose name turns out to be Freddy Freeman, but the boy is at the point of death. Captain Marvel takes him to the cave concealed beyond the disused subway tunnel where he can summon the wizard Shazam who originally endowed Captain Marvel with his power.

The wizard can't help the boy, but he indicates that Captain Marvel can save Freddy Freeman by bestowing the boy with some of his own power. Captain Marvel crouches over the dying boy and commands him, "Speak my name!"

"Why, it's Captain Marvel!"

The magic lightning crashes down and Freddy Freeman is transformed into Captain Marvel, Jr. He is a thirteen-or fourteen-year-old version of Marvel Sr., except his costume and cape are blue and gold rather than the red and white of Sr.'s. The bad news is that, when Captain Marvel, Jr. reverts to the Freddy Freeman identity, he becomes a crippled orphan, forced to sell newspapers outside the bank at the corner of Oak and Main.

In her book, *Elvis and Gladys,* Elaine Dundy attaches great significance to Elvis' Captain Marvel, Jr. fixation, feeling that the idea of the poor orphan boy who could turn himself at will into a super-powered being by invoking the name of an omnipotent male figure, struck a chord in Elvis, a shy kid raised in an environment where the father was weak and ineffectual, and the mother both dominated and fought for the survival of the family.

The story goes that, sometime around the age of twelve, Elvis read the Captain Marvel, Jr. issue titled "Atlantis Rises Again," and it would stick with him for the rest of his life. The comic book tale is described in *Elvis and Gladys:*

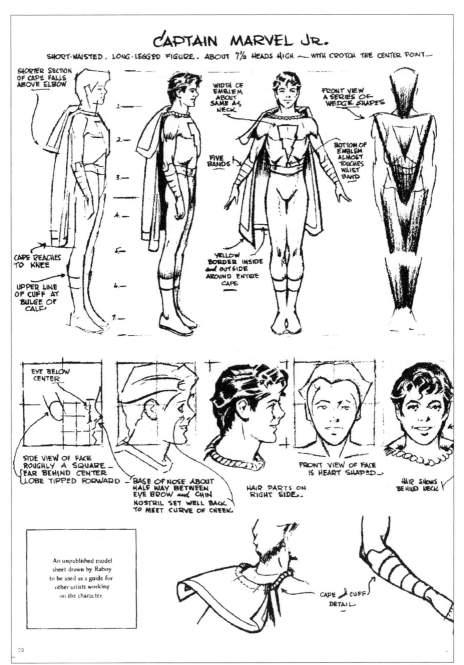

CAPTAIN MARVEL JR.

SHORT-WAISTED, LONG-LEGGED FIGURE. ABOUT 7½ HEADS HIGH — WITH CROTCH THE CENTER POINT —

SHORTER SECTION OF CAPE FALLS ABOVE ELBOW

WIDTH OF EMBLEM ABOUT SAME AS NECK

FRONT VIEW A SERIES OF WEDGE SHAPES

BOTTOM OF EMBLEM ALMOST TOUCHES WAIST BAND

FIVE BANDS

CAPE REACHES TO KNEE

UPPER LINE OF CUFF AT BULGE OF CALF

YELLOW BORDER INSIDE and OUTSIDE AROUND ENTIRE CAPE

EYE BELOW CENTER

SIDE VIEW OF FACE ROUGHLY A SQUARE
EAR BEHIND CENTER
LOBE TIPPED FORWARD

BASE OF NOSE ABOUT HALF WAY BETWEEN EYE BROW and CHIN
NOSTRIL SET WELL BACK TO MEET CURVE OF CHEEK

HAIR PARTS ON RIGHT SIDE.

FRONT VIEW OF FACE IS HEART SHAPED.

HAIR SHOWS BEHIND NECK

An unpublished model sheet drawn by Raboy to be used as a guide for other artists working on the character.

CAPE and CUFF DETAIL

Captain Marvel, Jr. has traveled forward in time to the thirteen- thousandth century. He is asked his name by Chass, a character in this future world. Captain Marvel, Jr. begins, "Why I'm Captain Mar...er... uh..." And then he halts. Why?

On the last panel on the page is the explanation: "Captain Marvel, Jr., alone of the Marvel family, always has a peculiar problem when people ask his name for..." And then Marvel, Jr. explains it to his readers in a thought balloon: It seems that whenever he says his name, the magic lightning comes and those words, "Captain Marvel," make him change back into poor Freddy Freeman! So he hesitates. However, as he is so far in the future, why not disclose his true powerful identity? What has he to lose?

"I'm Captain Marvel, Jr. of the twentieth century," he says.

Boom! More lightning zig-zags with the uttering of the two key words. For the telling of his name, he is transformed back into Freddy Freeman, the poor crippled newsboy.

Thirteen-thousandth century Chass is astonished. "What...What! There are two of you?"

"Yes," says Freddy, "you see we change back and forth by magic lightning. It's safe to tell you because this is far from the twentieth century! Nobody knows my secret back there."

In short, Elvis must be constantly on his guard against declaring himself to anyone, for if his outrageous secret were known, he would no longer be the Most Powerful Boy in the World.

Whether or not Elvis actually believed that he was a form of superhero—or a messianic figure appointed to perform some unique task—or if that's merely a case of over-speculation on the part of Elaine Dundy and others like her who attempt to put a metaphysical spin on the Elvis legend, is highly debatable. One thing is sure, however. In later life, Elvis would adopt a modified version of Captain Marvel, Jr.'s magic lightning symbol as his personal insignia to be worn by himself, his staff, and henchmen, like the badge of a private club. It would also be a major merchandising item after his death and a serious talisman for the faithful. *(See also ELVIS AND GLADYS and TCB.)*

Cave, Nick

On the 1985 album, *The Firstborn Is Dead (Mute-Homestead)*, Australian gothic rocker Nick Cave and his band The Bad Seeds made one of the first rock & roll forays into the idea that Elvis was a mythic entity, part of some darkly magical southern sub-culture that also includes voodoo and the blues. The title obviously refers to Jesse Garon Presley. Around the same time, Cave also recorded a strange grim version of "In The Ghetto." The lyrics of the "The Firstborn Is Dead" include the lines:

And the black rain came down,
Water water everywhere.

Where no bird can fly no fish can swim.
No fish can swim until the King is born!
Until the King is born! In Tupelo! In Tupelo!
Til the King is born in Tupelo!

Well Saturday gives what Sunday steals.
And a child is born on his brother's heels
Come Sunday morn the firstborn is dead,
In a shoebox tied with a ribbon of red.
Tupelo! Hey Tupelo!
In a shoebox tied with a ribbon of red!

The album is still on catalogue.

Celler, Emanuel

In 1957, New York Congressman Emanuel Celler, chairman of the Anti-trust
Subcommittee of the House Judiciary Committee that was investigating the
payola scandal in the record industry, stated that "while rock & roll has its
place and has given great impetus to talent, particularly among the coloured
people, the music of Elvis Presley and his animal gyrations are violative of all
we know to be good."

Charro!

Feature Film, 1969. Elvis Presley, Ina Balin,
Victor French, Lynn Kellogg, Barbara Werle.
Directed by Charles Marquis Warren.

Elvis' third western was an attempt to
restore his movie fortunes by casting him in a
straight spaghetti-style shoot 'em up that featured only one song and had Elvis wearing a
three-day growth of beard in the manner of
Clint Eastwood in the Sergio Leone "Dollars"
westerns. The posters proclaimed "A different kind of role...a different kind of man!"
Unfortunately, even the beard didn't help.
Elvis' stock by that point was so low in the
cinema that *Charro!* was released as a double
feature along with the Japanese creature epic
Ghidrah, The Three Headed Monster. It
bombed, but at the same time, its failure may have been a contributory factor
in motivating Elvis to concentrate on his return to live music.

Colour, 98 minutes. Available on videocassette.

Posters for *Charro!*, including French and Italian editions, show up in specialist movie and rock memorabilia stores more often than one would imagine,
considering the failure of the movie when it was first released.

Chenault's Restaurant

Memphis landmark at 1407 S. Bellevue Boulevard.

A favourite Memphis hangout of Elvis and his entourage. His practice was to rent the Chenault's Delta Room for parties thrown by himself and the Memphis Mafia.

Chi

The Jewish symbol of life that Elvis wore on a chain around his neck along with a Christian crucifix.

Chu-Bops

A slightly unusual bubble gum marketing project in which the gum was packaged in miniature reproduction record sleeves. Numbers 41 through 48 in the series featured Elvis albums—*Blue Hawaii, Elvis, Elvis Presley, G.I. Blues, From Elvis Presley Boulevard, Aloha From Hawaii, Something For Everybody,* and *Loving You.*

Chu-Bops were in mass distribution in the early eighties. Now they are strictly collectors' items. *(see also BUBBLE GUM.)*

Chuck E. Cheese's

Many of the Chuck E. Cheese's chain of amusement orientated pizza restaurants for children (where a kid can be a kid!) feature a life-size, performing robot Elvis.

Clinton, Bill

President Bill Clinton, coming as he did from Arkansas, just across the river from Memphis, was the first politician on a national level to realise the grassroots power that could be conjured by invoking the name and memory of Elvis Presley. Although the theme song of the Clinton campaign was Fleetwood Mac's "Don't Stop Thinking About Tomorrow," Elvis was constantly used as a reference point and a source of down-home credentials during Clinton's successful 1992 bid for the presidency, and campaign workers only stopped just short of actually making "Elvis" a nickname for their candidate.

Clinton made a point of appearing on TV to give his opinion on the "election" for the choice of the Elvis postage stamp (he went with the majority and favoured the image of the young Elvis). He also appeared as a musical guest on the late night talk show "Arsenio," sitting in with the house band on tenor saxophone for an instrumental version of "Heartbreak Hotel."

The nearest Clinton came to actually claiming the mantle of Elvishood was at the 1992 Democratic Convention in New York's Madison Square Garden, when Al Gore told the crowd that he had two ambitions in life—"to be elected

Vice President and to open for Elvis at the Garden." Gore seemed to be imply-
ing that he was about to achieve both in one fell swoop.

Clinton is also a great lover of junk food. *(see also STAMP.)*

Clock

In 1992, an Elvis clock came on the market. Essentially
it was a flat cutout of Elvis, some nine inches high in a
pose from his performance of "Hound Dog" on the
Milton Berle Show. The electric clock mechanism was
geared so Elvis' free hanging, articulated legs moved in
a rough approximation of his fifties stage gyrations. On
the original (and fairly expensive) Graceland autho-
rised models, the figure of Elvis was outlined by a cus-
tom shaped neon tube. Almost immediately, however,
cheap knockoffs started appearing without the neon
surround. Inside of two years, these had totally satu-
rated the market and Elvis clocks can now be found in
discount and cutout stores for next to nothing. This
story has been the typical lifecycle of a lot of Elvis merchandise.

Other, less elaborate Elvis clocks have also been
marketed using standard clock designs with inset photographs of Elvis, the Elvis stamp, etc....

Coffee mugs

The number of different designs of coffee mugs that carry either the name or
image of Elvis must now easily run into the hundreds. Check the Elvis section
of any "hip" giftshop and you'll probably find at least a half-dozen. One set of
Elvis coffee mugs carries pictures of the cars that he owned.

Colgate

Elvis' favourite brand of toothpaste.

Collectors Tin & Card Set

A 1994 item from the Graceland gift catalogue. "Twenty metal-encased cards
include images of Elvis on stage and glamour shots. Beautifully decorated stor-
age tin. Imported. Perfect gift!" In other words, another fifty buck item to add
to the general Elvis clutter.

Available from Graceland Gifts, 1-800-238-2000.

Colonel

Elvis had quite as much right to refer to himself as Colonel as Tom Parker did. The honorary rank was conferred on him by Tennessee Governor Buford Ellington in 1961.

Complete Elvis, The

Large format paperback book, 1982. Edited by Martin Torgoff: Delilah Books.

Despite the title, this collection of lists, information, souvenirs, and trivia was anything but complete.

Out of print.

Contents of Elvis' stomach

The autopsy of Elvis conducted at Baptist Memorial Hospital in Memphis revealed traces of the following medications in Elvis' stomach at the time of his death—Codeine (in high concentration), Morphine, Quaaludes, Valium, Valmid, Placidyl, Amytal, Nembutal, Demerol and Sinutab. *(see also DEATH OF ELVIS, THE and DRUGS.)*

Cosmetics

Elvis Presley Lipstick (colours included Hound Dog Orange, Tender Pink, Heartbreak Pink, Love-ya Fuschia, Tutti-Frutti Red, Cruel Red)—1956; Elvis Presley Love Me Tender Path Products—1985; Elvis Cologne—1991; The King Cologne—1992.

No less than four attempts have been made over the years to market Elvis Presley cosmetic products. None were such an overwhelming success that they caused Revlon or Chanel to lose any sleep. The problem in every case was that, although the packaging was pure Elvis, the products themselves weren't of a quality to make it beyond the level of a novelty item. The first, the lipsticks, man-ufactured under license in 1956 during the first flush of Elvismania, have van-ished from the face of the Earth, and to find one today would require tenacious pop archeology and considerable luck.

Love Me Tender Milk Bath and Love Me Tender Bubble Bath appeared on the market in 1985. Packaged in one-pint, gold plastic bottles and adorned with a full colour painting of Elvis that wouldn't have looked out of place on the cover of a romance novel (the original, life size oil hangs in Graceland), they were intended to spearhead an entire line of Elvis beauty products that never actually materialised. They still show up in stores that specialise in rock & roll collectibles.

Elvis cologne—"for all the King's men"—was marketed through drug store chains in the summer of 1991 in a gift package with a free Elvis coffee mug. Unfortunately, the actual fragrance, designed by Irwin Goldberg, left a lot to be desired. The King cologne that came out in time for Christmas 1992 was a trifle intense but not unacceptable. In a rectangular black glass bottle like a miniature monolith, it has come closest so far to being a workable fragrance.

During his life, Elvis himself used Brut 33 by Faberge. Hound Dog Pink Lipstick is virtually unobtainable. Love Me Tender Bubble Bath was manufactured by Natural Choice Industries Inc., Westlake Village, CA 91362, and is occasionally available from Wacko, 7402 Melrose Ave., Los Angeles, CA 90046. Elvis Cologne is marketed by Trends Inc., and sold through major drugstore chains. The King cologne is manufactured by Elvis Fragrances Inc., Atlanta, GA 30339, and distributed by Home Shopping Club, St. Petersburg, FL 33716.

Credit cards

During the eighties, a Tennessee bank issued a credit card bearing a picture of Elvis. Unfortunately these are now discontinued.

Cross-stitch kits

Either these are for the really bored or they're a sign that Elvis fans are growing progressively older. These kits contain everything a body could need to sew a beautiful, ready-for-framing sampler of either Graceland or Elvis himself in a famous pose from the fifties. Ever get the feeling that parts of the Elvis Universe are expanding in some decidedly strange directions?

Available from needlework and hobby stores.

Crown Electric

Memphis landmark at 353 Poplar Avenue.

The building at which Elvis worked for a little over a buck-and-a-quarter per hour prior to cutting his first record for Sun, is now occupied by B&H Hardware.

Crudup, Arthur (Big Boy)

Arthur "Big Boy" Crudup was a well known blues shouter of the late forties and early fifties whose raucous R&B style was a formative musical influence on the youthful Elvis Presley, to the point that a Crudup tune "That's All Right" was chosen as his first release on Sun Records. Elvis also recorded "My Baby Left Me" and "So Glad Your Mine," both Crudup tunes. Later in life, Elvis would finance recording sessions for Fire Records when Crudup had fallen on hard times.

Elvis himself recalled—"Sam Phillips suggested over the phone, 'You want to make some blues?' I'd always been a sucker for that kind of jive. He mentioned Big Boy Crudup's name and maybe others too. All I know is, I hung up and ran 15 blocks to Mr. Phillips' office before he'd gotten off the line—or so he tells me. We talked about the Crudup numbers I knew—'Cool Disposition,' 'Rock Me Mama,' 'Hey Mama,' 'Everything's All Right,' and others, but I settled for 'That's All Right.'"

Dead Elvis

Hardback book, 1991. By Greil Marcus: Doubleday.

Greil Marcus is a leading figure among the academic establishment of American rock critics. This book is a collection of his writings that span the period between Elvis' death and the book's publication, and deals, in the main, with various kinds of Elvis obsession—the mythology, the mysticism, the legends and rumours, the confused relationship between punk rock and Elvis. It also has a liberal sprinkling of illustrations, mainly examples of the more left-field areas of Elvis graphics. The book is a little thin in content, tends to be a little too cut up, and as a collection of previous writing, it continuously shifts perspective. It is, however, a brave and grand attempt to look head on at the weirdness that surrounds Elvis. Marcus unfortunately draws no conclusions, except that we may never decipher Elvis. And in this, he may well be absolutely correct.

Still available in bookstores.

Dear Elvis

Magazine column, 1963.

The January 1963 issue of *TV & Movie Screen* featured an advice column supposedly written by Elvis. Copies of the magazine are now rare collectors' items.

Death of Elvis, The

Paperback book, 1992. By Charles C. Thompson and James P. Cole: Dell Paperback.

A highly detailed account by two Memphis reporters of Elvis' death, the events that followed and the attempts to cover up or gloss over his serious drug problems. Although hardly a scintillating read, the book is scrupulous in its detail and ultimately lays to rest any serious claim that Elvis might be alive.

Available from bookshops or Dell Readers, Box DR, 666 Fifth Avenue, New York, NY 10103.

Denim jacket

The eighties fad for embroidered or otherwise decorated denim jackets saw the creation of a large number decorated with portraits of Elvis. They were, however, far from cheap—in some cases running hundreds of dollars. The Graceland gift catalogue currently carries a machine embroidered version for just over a hundred bucks.

Available from Graceland Gifts, 1-800-238-2000.

Divorce

The divorce was finalized between Elvis and Priscilla on 9 October 1973. Priscilla walked out of the Santa Monica courthouse with custody of Lisa Marie, a lump sum of $2 million, $6,000 a month for ten years, $4,200 a month alimony for one year, $4,000 a month child support, $25,000 from the sale of their Los Angeles home, and five percent of two of Elvis' music publishing companies. Perhaps not a bad deal considering that she ran off with the karate instructor.

Dolls

Nineteen fifty-seven saw the marketing of the first Elvis doll. Billed as the "only doll officially approved by Elvis Presley," the smiling oddity was eighteen inches tall and dressed in blue suede shoes, blue jeans, and a plaid shirt with an upturned collar. It was "perfectly proportioned" (although in pictures, the head looks unnaturally large and featured "long, wavy hair moulded hair and sideburns." It sold for $3.98 and the advertising copy warned that "when your friends see your Elvis doll, they'll want to tear it out of your hands, so be prepared. Hang on tight."

Such dolls are now a very rare collectors item.

A line of Elvis dolls was marketed on TV in 1994—three models: an early rockabilly Elvis in sportcoat and string tie holding a guitar; a later fifties version in red windbreakers and white shoes, also holding a guitar; and a 1968 leather-suited Elvis with microphone and stand instead of a guitar. All three dolls were mounted on plastic display stands. The merchandising campaign was fairly short-lived and later in '94, the same dolls started turning up in drugstores and toyshops.

Donner, Ral

Ral Donner was one of the most accurate and successful of all the Elvis sound-a-likes of the fifties and sixties. He had two hits in his own right, "You Don't Know What You Got" and "Girl Of My Best Friend." In 1981, he did the voice-over narration for the movie *This Is Elvis*. Ral Donner died of cancer in 1984.

Doors, Inc.

The world famous wrought-iron gates of Graceland were constructed and installed in 1957 by Doors, Inc. of 911 Rayner Street, Memphis.

Dors, Diana

Diana Dors, "the blonde bombshell," was England's surrogate Marilyn Monroe. She first met Elvis at a party in 1956. After Elvis died, Dors—by then a British national institution not unlike Shelley Winters in the U.S.—revealed in a story in the London *Sunday Mirror*, titled "Elvis Was My Love" that she had made love to Elvis on numerous occasions; that he had given her a Pink Cadillac; and that on a weekend in Mexico, she and Elvis had smoked marijuana.

Drugs

According to one legend, Elvis was first turned on to amphetamines by a sergeant during his stint in the Army. An alternate story is that Elvis was already popping pills when he was out on the road with Scotty Moore and Bill Black during the Sun Records era, and that his mother's constant battle with her weight gave Elvis a ready source of speed-based diet pills. Certainly, after the Army, members of the Memphis Mafia have recounted how Elvis used various kinds of amphetamines in order to get his weight down before he was scheduled to shoot a movie. The speed kept him awake, however, so he also took barbiturates in order to sleep. This was the cycle that would escalate relentlessly through the rest of his life and ultimately kill him.

Ellis, Jimmy

(see ORION.)

El Vez

Elvis impersonator.

Although he is frequently characterised as an "Elvis impersonator," performance artist Robert Lopez goes a great deal further than any of the overweight guys who make a living or gratify a need for attention by dressing up in jumpsuit, sideburns, and sunglasses. El Vez is a bizarre and inspired creation in which Elvis has become a kitsch-crazed Latino performing songs like "Huaraches Azul," "En El Barrio," and "Viva Le Raza" backed by the Memphis Mariachi Band and girl singers, the Elvettes. His extensive and flamboyant wardrobe includes a white, double-knit polyester jumpsuit with red, white, and green rhinestones and a sequinned Virgin of Guadalupe on the back.

Originally the curator of an avant garde Los Angeles art gallery, Lopez conceived the El Vez concept as a part of a 1988 exhibition of Elvis "overkill." Subsequently, El Vez took his show to that year's Elvis Tribute Week in Memphis, where he performed both in front of Graceland and at Bad Bob's nightclub. Traditionalist Elvis fans were far from amused, and Lopez barely escaped with his life. Undeterred, however, El Vez continues to this day, weirdly bridging the gap between the art world and Elvis fans. On January 8, 1993, he contributed to the celebrations that marked the issue of the Elvis postage stamp by performing at the main Hollywood Post Office on Wilcox Avenue.

When asked by a TV reporter how long this "Elvis thing" was going to go on, El Vez simply replied "Better get used to it, Paco. It's going to go on to infinity."

El Vez can be contacted at 2254 Fargo Street, Los Angeles, CA 90039. Phone: 213-666-2927.

Elvis (name)

The name Elvis is most usually accepted to have been derived from the Norse word "alviss," meaning "all wise."

Elvis (rose)

Elvis was the name given to a small red rose hybridized in 1981 by W.W. (Whit) Wells, a member of the American Rose society.

Elvis (book)

Hardback and paperback book, 1981. By Albert Goldman: McGraw Hill/Avon.

This long awaited biography of Elvis by the author of *Ladies And Gentlemen—Lenny Bruce* caused dismay and fury among both Elvis fans and serious rock critics when it was published in 1981. Based largely on the memoirs of Memphis Mafia member Lamar Fike, it is lengthy and heavily researched, but the facts are so distorted by the overbearing prejudice of the author and his clear contempt for both his specific subject and pop culture in general that it is rendered quite worthless as the serious work it purports to be. When the book was first published, guerrilla groups of Elvis fans, copying radical feminist actions against offensive advertising, hit bookstores, plastering unsold copies of the book with stickers bearing the slogan "THIS BOOK DEGRADES ELVIS."

Goldman would later repeat the whole process with a biography of John Lennon. Critic James Tamarkin possibly made the most succinct summation of Goldman's *Elvis*. "Perhaps no book about rock 'n' roll has been as maligned as Goldman's exhaustive Elvis bio, and deservedly so."

The book is still in print.

Elvis (movie)

TV movie, 1979 (released theatrically in Europe). Kurt Russell, Shelley Winters, Pat Hingle, Season Hubley. Directed by John Carpenter.

If there was only one Elvis Presley bio-pic in the world, this might as well be the one (Although it does stop with his return to the Vegas stage in 1969, and doesn't tackle the more thorny narrative of his decline and fall.) Directed by horror master John Carpenter, and surrounded by a strong supporting cast, Kurt Russell manages to achieve the near-impossible task of suspending the audience's disbelief and convincing them in short order that he is Elvis for the duration of the movie. The songs were dubbed by Elvis sound-a-like Ronnie McDowell. *Elvis* is one of the highest rated TV movies ever, beating out a

highly promoted rerun of *Gone With The Wind* on its first airing.
Available on videocassette.

Elvis (TV Series)

TV series, 1990. Michael St. Gerard, Millie Perkins, Billy Greenbush, Jesse Dabson, Blake Gibbons.

The prefame Elvis, living at home with his parents, out on the road for the first time with Scotty and Bill, and ultimately cutting his first records for Sun are all lovingly recreated in this well-made ABC TV series that is still one of the finest pieces of product to come out under the auspices of the Elvis Presley Estate.

Unfortunately, just ten episodes of the show were aired before being was canceled by the network. "Elvis" had the sheer bad luck to find itself programmed on Sunday nights in the same time slot as "The Simpsons" on Fox that, back in 1990 was in the process of becoming a runaway hit and a national institution. Elvis fans actually shouldn't be too upset about this seemingly failed show. When Fox moved "The Simpsons" to Thursday night, it also aced out long-running and seemingly impregnable "The Cosby Show."

Turner Broadcasting has recently started airing "Elvis" as part of Elvis marathons celebrating Elvis' birthday.

Michael St. Gerard had played Elvis once before, as a bit part in the awful Jerry Lee Lewis biopic *Great Balls Of Fire*. Billy Green Bush had also played Vernon before in *Elvis*, the movie. Millie Perkins (who played Gladys) had appeared with the real Elvis as one of his girlfriends in *Wild In The Country*, and years before that, she had co-starred in *The Diary Of Anne Frank* with Shelley Winters, who played Gladys in *Elvis* the movie. Something to think about, right?

Not yet available on videocassette.

Elvis – A Biography

Hardback and paperback book, 1971. By Jerry Hopkins: Simon and Schuster/Warner Books.

Written at the instigation of Jim Morrison, *Rolling Stone* writer Jerry Hopkins not only produced the first serious biography of Elvis Presley but also a work that has stood the test of time and remains one of the best reference works on the subject. *(see also ELVIS – THE FINAL YEARS.)*

The book is still in print.

Elvis and Gladys

Hardback book, 1985. By Elaine Dundy: Dell.

One of the better books written about Elvis. A heavily researched account of Elvis growing up in Tupelo and a thoughtful examination of his unique rela-

tionship with his mother. *(see also CAPTAIN MARVEL, JR.)*
Out of print but can be found in second-hand bookstores.

Elvis and Kathy

Hardback book, 1987. By Kathy Westmoreland: Glendale House.
Kiss and tell volume by Kathy Westmoreland, one of Elvis' back-up singers through the 1970s. *(see also WESTMORELAND, KATHY.)*

Elvis and Me (book)

Hardback and paperback book, 1985. By Priscilla Beaulieu Presley with Sandy Harmon: Putnam/Berkeley.
The ultimate kiss-and-tell bio by Elvis' ex-wife. A massive best seller that would be made into a TV mini-series. *(see also PRESLEY, PRISCILLA.)*

Elvis and Me (TV mini-series)

TV mini-series, 1988. Susan Walters, Dale Midkiff, Billy Greenbush. Directed by Larry Peerce.
A run-of-the-mill soap opera-style adaptation of Priscilla Presley's book of the same name. The show wasn't enhanced by Dale Midkiff's barely marginal resemblance to Elvis. Once again, the songs were dubbed by Ronnie McDowell.
Available on videocassette.

Elvis and the Beauty Queen

TV movie, 1981. Don Johnson, Stephanie Zimbalist, Rick Lenz, Ann Wedgeworth. Directed by Gus Trikonis
Who could ever forget the pre-"Miami Vice" Don Johnson playing Elvis? On the other hand, who would really want to remember? A Sunday night made-for-TV piece of exploitation based on the five-year affair between Elvis and Linda Thompson. Stephanie Zimbalist played Linda and the songs were dubbed by Ronnie McDowell.
100 minutes. Not available on videocassette.

Elvis and the Colonel (book)

Hardback and paperback book, 1988. By Dirk Vellenga and Mick Farren: Dell.
Exhaustively researched and brilliantly written biography of Colonel Tom Parker that seeks to prove that he was a grasping conniving lowlife who, after the initial blaze of fame and fortune, did considerable damage to Elvis' life and career.
Still in print.

Elvis and the Colonel (TV movie)

TV movie, 1993. Beau Bridges: Dick Clark Productions.

Cheap exploitative TV biopic of the Colonel. Only the title was borrowed from the fine book of the same name. First broadcast 10 January, 1993, the Sunday night following Elvis' birthday and the issue of the Elvis stamp.

Not available on videocassette.

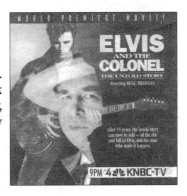

Elvis Aaron Presley Highway

Landmark.

This 104 mile stretch of Highway 78 was the route taken by Vernon Presley when he moved his family from Tupelo to Memphis in 1948. It was renamed in December 1977, just five months after Elvis' death.

Elvis Collectibles

Large format paperback book, 1991. By Rosalie Cranor: Overmountain Press.

Now Elvis paraphernalia has entered the collectible world along with comic books and baseball cards with "experts" and price guides and the rest of the trappings of unfettered commercialism. This is the basic bible.

Available in bookstores.

Elvis Collection, The

Trading cards, 1993.

The Elvis Collection was launched with heavy promotion and TV advertising. When boiled down, however, it amounted to nothing more than a set of twelve to a pack, well printed, full colour, bubble gum cards without the gum. For a while, they were prominently displayed in the impulse buy areas near the checkout at drugstores and supermarkets. After a while, however, they began to disappear, leading to the assumption that they had failed to grab the public's fancy. Part of the problem was that the cards lacked any particularly unusual images of Elvis that we hadn't been previously seen. But let us not forget that today's failed commercial venture can often be tomorrow's collectors' item.

Still available in specialist trading card stores.

Elvis Cover-Up, The

TV show, 1979.

As a part of the long-running ABC magazine show "20/20," Geraldo Rivera made one of the first investigations into Elvis' death that revealed his drug use and the efforts that had been made in Memphis to cover up the facts. The show first aired on 13 September 1979.

Elvis '56 – In the Beginning

Large format paperback book, 1977. By Alfred Wertheimer.

In 1956, photographer Alfred Wertheimer traveled with Elvis from Memphis to New York (for the "The Ed Sullivan Show") and back again, shooting some 3,800 pictures in the process, some of which were nothing short of brilliant. This is an elegantly printed collection of the very best. My particular favourite is the one of a jewelry salesman showing Elvis a selection of diamond rings in his dressing room at the Ed Sullivan Theatre.

Elvis '56 – In The Beginning can still be found in specialist and second hand bookstores.

Elvis '56

TV documentary, 1987. Directed by Alan and Susan Raymond. Cinemax.

This excellent cable TV documentary, narrated by Levon Helm of The Band, is one of the best documentaries ever produced about Elvis at his 1950s, rock & roll best, chronicling as it does the year in which Elvis rose to full international stardom. It includes live clips from "Stage Show," "The Milton Berle Show," and "The Ed Sullivan Show," plus rostrum work based on the photographs of Alfred Wertheimer.

The show was first aired on 16 August 1987, the first anniversary of Elvis' death.

Available on videocassette.

Elvis – His Life from A to Z

Hardback book, 1992. By Fred L. Worth and Steve D. Tamerius: Wings Books.

This massive volume, over 600 pages, is the closest that we have come to a full scale Elvis encyclopedia. Exhaustive in its research and detail and maintaining a superior level of accuracy, its authors have to be respected, even in this on-line computer age, for the sheer volume of pain and labour involved.

Available at bookstores.

Elvis – Images and Fancies

Book, 1981. Edited by Jack L. Tharpe: University Of Mississippi.

The first academic study of Elvis, focusing on Elvis worship and the fans. The book can be obtained from the University.

Elvis In His Own Words

Trade paperback book, 1977. By Mick Farren and Pearce Marshbank: Omnibus Press.

Heavily illustrated, elegantly designed, and beautifully put together, this volume contains transcripts of all of Elvis' major public utterances.

Previously out of print, reissued June 1994.

Elvis on Black Velvet

The truck stops and motels of rural America are some of the greatest sources in the world of Elvis folk art. Traditionally, the truckstop and the "mom and pop" motel have always been places where local craft items and produce have been offered for sale. In Maine, one would find seashell statues and carved driftwood, while in Arizona or New Mexico, the traveler might be offered dinosaur fossils or Indian beadwork. Amateur paintings of wildly varying quality were always a part of this down-home free enterprise—elaborately romantic desert sunsets or horses galloping through the surf abounded.

As mass culture increasingly homogenized the country, noble portraits of John Wayne and John Kennedy became a regular feature of these exhibits. After his death, it was inevitable that Elvis should also become an major icon in this kind of commercial folk-art portraiture. It was around the same time that the use of dayglo paint on black velvet also enjoyed a blue collar vogue with paintings of clowns, big eyed kittens, Indian maidens, jungle scenes, heraldic panthers, and even flying saucers and extra-terrestrial landscapes. From 1977 onwards, Elvis was right there as a constant in this array of neo-folk imagery, and now it's hard to find any of these unofficial art galleries without a full complement of Elvis on black velvet.

Elvis People – The Cult of the King

Trade paperback, 1992. By Ted Harrison: Harpers Collins/Fount.

To actually come out and suggest that Elvis worship is turning into some kind of religious cult has been to invite the kind of look reserved for those who have crossed the line into stone insanity. What makes *Elvis People – The Cult Of The King* so interesting is that it comes roaring out of left field and says exactly that and fears no ridicule. Metaphysics, you see, are Ted Harrison's business. Far from being some crazed Elvis fanatic, he's a British religious writer and broadcaster and he knows a theological phenomenon when he sees one.

"Over the centuries, many cults and religions have been started. The Elvis cult is one of the latest. There are emperors who have been worshipped, saints, gurus, charlatans, and even pets who have been the focus of devotion. Each cult has been a product of its time and nurturing society."

Harrison points out that there is something fundamentally unique about whatever now surrounds Elvis. Many artists have been respected over the centuries, but none have achieved such cult status. "Cults and new religions only form around a prophet or personality whose projected image and sustaining aura feeds a spiritual hunger."

Available in bookstores.

Elvis Presley

Bio-comic, 1992. By Tiki and Delmo Waters: Personality Classics.

A uninspired piece of exploitation in a series that includes John Wayne, John Lennon, and Madonna.

Available in comic book stores.

Elvis Presley Boulevard Sign

If for no other reason than to prevent the theft of the real ones, reproductions of the street signs for Elvis Presley Boulevard—full size, with white lettering on green—have been a longtime Elvis souvenir particularly in Memphis, where they're sold to the tourists.

A miniature of the sign is also marketed as a enamel pin.

Available in souvenir stores and at the Memphis airport.

Elvis Presley Day

No less that 13 states have declared an official Elvis Presley Day since 1956. Governor George Wallace of Alabama went one better—he declared Elvis Presley Week in March of 1964.

Elvis Presley Game

Board Game.

A board game marketed in 1957 was one of the earliest pieces of Elvis merchandising. Promoted as "a party game for the Tender of Heart," the concept was, to say the least, a strange one. Elvis was used in the role of a fortune-telling oracle for "Love, Romance and Marriage." In many respects, it was equated Elvis to the Magic 8-Ball.

This is an extremely rare item, and should you find one in the attic, it's probably worth a fortune.

Elvis Presley – Hero or Heel

Magazine format book, 1956. Publisher unknown.

Despite the dramatic title, this magazine-style "book" had pretty much made up its mind that Elvis was a hero, although it did pay some scant lip service to the school of thought that Elvis was obscene and rock & roll was the music of Satan. It was essentially a newsstand and supermarket impulse buy, a

Elvis Presley bio-comic

Elvis Presley Day

piece of exploitation aimed directly at Elvis fans. Lavishly illustrated, it did however, constitute what, in hindsight was a fabulous collection of early photos of Elvis.

Now a rare collectors' item.

Elvis Presley Museum, The

Landmarks.

In addition to Graceland itself and his birthplace in Tupelo, at least two Elvis Presley museums exist today.

The museum founded by singer Jimmy Velvet in 1979 is directly across the street from Graceland at 3350 Elvis Presley Boulevard. It contains six Elvis-related cars, his Harley, his wedding album, his family Bible, and a considerable number of costumes, watches and jewelry.

Billing itself as the "World's Largest Private Collection of Elvis Memorabilia," this museum run by Mike L. Moon in Pidgeon Forge, Tennessee, boasts a number of cars and some jewelry. Essentially it is a souvenir store with some permanent exhibits.

Elvis Presley Plaza

Memphis Landmark.

This open area just south of downtown Memphis is home to the bronze Elvis Presley statue by Eric Parks and is dedicated to the memory of Elvis. It was established in 1980.

Courtesy Memphis Tourist Development

Elvis Presley Speaks

Paperback book, 1978. By Hans Holzer: Manor Books.

Psychic Hans Holzer is in touch with Elvis on the other side. Unfortunately Elvis doesn't have much to say beyond some dopey platitudes. Maybe this is what happens to you when you're dead.

More a quirk than a collectors' item. Hard to find, but you might get lucky at a secondhand bookstore.

Elvis Presley Story, The

Paperback book, 1960. Edited by James Gregory, introduction by Dick Clark: Hillman Books.

A 35 cent fan book that now sells for $25.

Rare but obtainable.

Elvis Room, The

In the eighties and nineties, the Elvis shrines that many hard-core fans had maintained since—or, in some cases, even before—Elvis' death grew so large that they took up entire rooms. The phenomena of the Elvis Room came into being—an entire room in a fan's home, devoted to his or her idol, that served not only as a shrine but also what amounted to a place of meditation. At the rate in which the Elvis Estate is licensing all manner of Elvis junk, the truly devoted fan will, very soon, have to enlarge the Elvis Room into the Elvis Extension to the house.

Elvis' Greatest Shit!

Bootleg album, 1984. Dog Vomit Label (Sux 005)

This infamous and lavishly packaged record, with the *National Enquirer* photo of Elvis in his coffin on the front cover, is a dubious classic, including as it does, some of the absolute worst of Elvis Presley. The tracks are...

"Old McDonald Had A Farm"
"Ito Eats"
"There's No Room To Rhumba In A Sportscar"
"Confidence"
"Yoga Is As Yoga Does"
"Song Of The Shrimp"
"U.S. Male"
"Fort Lauderdale Chamber Of Commerce"
"Signs Of The Zodiac"
"The Bullfighter Was A Lady"
"Wolf Call"
"Can't Help Falling In Love"
"He's Your Uncle Not Your Dad"
"Scratch My Back Then I'll Scratch Yours"
"The Walls Have Ears"
"Poison Ivy League"
"Beach Boy Blues"
"Dominic The Impotent Bull"
"Queenie Wahine's Papaya"
"Do The Clambake"
"Datin'"
"Are You Lonesome Tonight (Incoherent live version)"

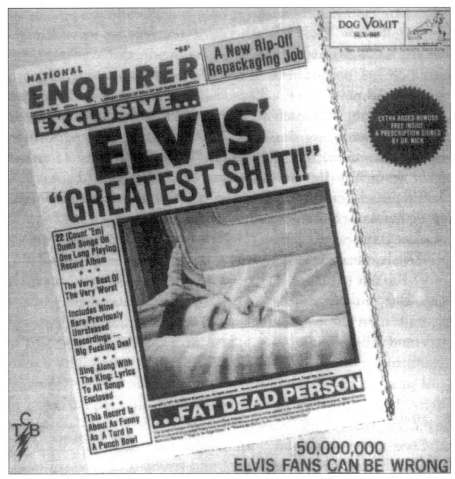

To listen to the entire album in a single sitting is an eerie and profoundly disturbing experience. How could an artist with so much talent record so much garbage? The surprise, until listening to the record, is the inclusion of "Can't Help Falling In Love." But upon listening to Elvis power his way through the classic ballad, you find out why. It's an outtake—Elvis loses the beat and curses, "Aw shiiiit!" After ten years, this record is still about. I've even heard tell of a CD version.

Elvis' Midget Fan Club

A typically tasteless Colonel Tom Parker publicity stunt from 1957, when the Colonel hired a team of midgets to parade through Memphis as part of an Elvis hometown promotion.

Elvis – The Final Years

Hardback and paperback book, 1980. By Jerry Hopkins: St. Martin's

Press/Berkeley.

Writer Jerry Hopkins' second book about Elvis in which he gets to finish the story that he began in his excellent *Elvis – A Biography*.

Elvis – The Illustrated Record

Large format hardback/paperback book. By Roy Carr and Mick Farren: Harmony Books.

A complete (to the year of publication), and highly detailed chronicle and analysis of Elvis' recording career. Lavishly illustrated.

Unfortunately out of print.

Elvis The King

The Franklin Mint got into the Elvis portrait business, and in a big way. In 1994, the well-known merchandisers of the deluxe Monopoly board and the Star Trek chess set came out with a mail-order offer of a framed Elvis print titled *Elvis The King* by Nate Giorgio, the artist responsible for a number of the Bradford Exchange Elvis plates. *Elvis The King* was touted as "The first hand-signed, limited edition, fine-art print of its kind, framed in luxurious hardwood, matted in genuine blue suede, emblazoned with the official seal of Graceland in a specially minted proof-quality coin lavished with rich accents of 24-karat gold."

The bad news is that the whole deal costs close to $200 by the time that you've made all the payments. *(see ELVIS ON BLACK VELVET.)*

Available from The Franklin Mint, 2710 Franklin Center, PA 19092-2710.

Elvis – The Paperdoll Book

Large format paperback book, 1982. By Jim Fitzgerald with artwork by Al Kilgore: St. Martin's Press.

Dress Elvis in dozens of cutout costumes and outfits.

Out of print, but does show up in collectors stores now and again.

Elvis Undercover

Comic book, 1987. By Tom Mason and Don Lomax: Mad Dog Graphics.

A parody action comic that chronicles Elvis' adventures as an undercover narcotics agent, based on an idea generated by the schpeil Elvis gave President Nixon when he wanted a narc badge. The comic was withdrawn before it hit the newsstands. Publisher Jan Strand was apparently warned off the project by the ghost of Elvis. *(see also NIXON, RICHARD MILHOUSE.)*

Elvis – What Happened?

Paperback book, 1977. By Red West, Sonny West and Dave Hebler with Steve Dunleavy: Ballantine.

The joke might be "how many of the Memphis Mafia does it take to write a book?" except that there was nothing particularly humourous about, *Elvis – What Happened.*

The West cousins were high school buddies of Elvis who were placed on the Presley payroll after Elvis came out of the Army in 1960. According to legend, during their school days Red West had saved Elvis from being beaten up by a crew of jocks who thought Elvis' long hair made him look like a sissy. Both were part of the longtime inner circle of the Memphis Mafia. Dave Hebler arrived on the scene considerably later. The former karate instructor became one of Elvis' bodyguards when he went back on the road in the early seventies. All three were understandably bitter when they were arbitrarily fired by Vernon Presley on 13 July 1976, apparently after a paranoid freakout on the part of Elvis.

Seemingly the book was not only a means to make a buck while unemployed, but also an act of media revenge on Elvis, who from the West's point of view had treated them extremely shabbily after what amounted to a lifetime in his service. While the book was being written, Elvis offered his ex-retainers their old jobs back and $50,000 each in cash if they'd drop the project. The Wests and Hebler refused, and book went ahead.

The shattering, below-the-belt exposé of Elvis' private life, including his tantrums, his sex life, and his drug habits was published on 1 August 1977. The timing couldn't have been more obscenely perfect. Two weeks later, Elvis was dead and the entire world was asking the very question that was the book's title: *Elvis – What happened?* The initial print run for *Elvis – What Happened?* had been a healthy 400,000 copies. On the day Elvis died, a further quarter-of-a-million were quickly printed. A week later, the K-Mart chain put in an order for two million books, which is still the largest retail book order ever placed.

Also referred to by Elvis scholars as the bodyguard book, *Elvis – What Happened?* was the first indication ever received by the public that Elvis, at the end of his life, was anything but the All American Boy of their imaginings.

Steve Dunleavy is now senior editor of the tabloid TV show "A Current Affair." On screen, he regularly demonstrates an aggressive contempt for Elvis. *(see also WEST, RED & SONNY.)*

Still in print.

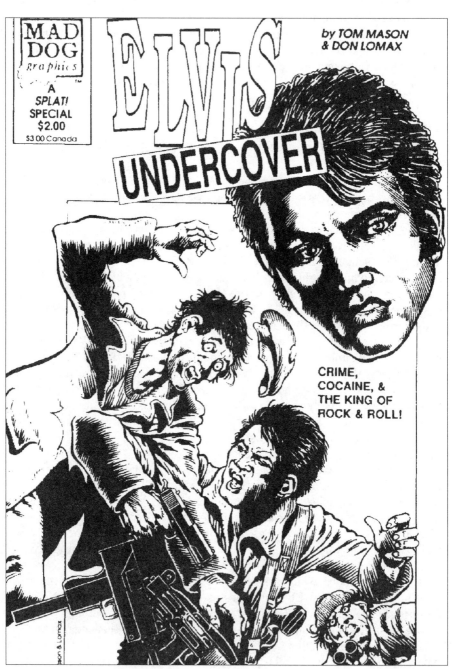

© Mad Dog Graphics

EP Continentals

Elvis World

Quarterly magazine.

Published out of Memphis, *Elvis World* is a well-respected publication among Elvis fans.

EP Continentals

The EP Continentals was one of the earliest of Elvis fan clubs. The club was named for Elvis' car of the moment. Any artifacts relating to the club—buttons, membership cards, etc., would now be worth a fortune.

Esposito, Joe

"Diamond" Joe Esposito was originally an Army buddy of Elvis who went to work for him when they both got out of the military in 1960. Esposito would seem to have been the closest and most highly paid of Elvis' hired henchman, and the unofficial leader of the Memphis Mafia. He was responsible for, among other things, deciding what women had access to Elvis.

On the night Elvis died, it was Esposito who summoned emergency services and also the one who informed Priscilla that Elvis was dead.

Joe Esposito, who is in the course of preparing his own book about Elvis that allegedly tells all about the women in Elvis' life, turns up regularly on TV talk shows with Elvis-related topics. *(see MEMPHIS MAFIA, THE.)*

Everett, Vince

Vince Everett was originally the name given to Elvis' character in the movie "Jailhouse Rock." It was later adopted by sound-a-like singer Marvin Benefield, who had a minor hit in 1963 with the tune "Baby Let's Play House" (ABC Paramount 10472). On the record, he was backed by Elvis' original back-up band—Scotty Moore, Bill Black and D.J. Fontana.

Facelift

Elvis underwent a facelift at Mid South Hospital in Memphis on 15 June 1975.

Face on Mars, The

Fan Theory circa 1988.

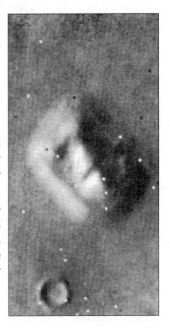

The feature on the planet Mars photographed by the Mariner Orbiter that bears an uncanny resemblance to a human face has been claimed by Elvis fans who firmly believe that it is a huge, mountain-sized sculpture of The King that proves that Elvis is an interplanetary entity, incarnated on different planets at different times. A variation of the same idea appeared as a cover story in the 20 September 1988 edition of the tabloid weekly the *Sun*. *(see also ALIENS.)*

Falcone, Bill

At the Berkeley Psychic Institute, also known as the Church of The Divine Man for a period in 1987, clairvoyant Bill Falcone repeatedly "channeled" Elvis from beyond the grave. In one of these sessions, Elvis provided a bizarre insight into the nature of the spiritual relationship with his twin Jesse Garon, and how they may have been two halves of a single being, supposedly the reason for the many contradictions in Elvis' personality.

"Elvis and his brother struggled for control of the surviving body. Elvis the Rebel (the Jesse spirit) wore sideburns and wild pink and black clothes and worshipped James Dean. Elvis the Good Boy (the original spirit) was deeply religious. The struggle between the two spirits in Elvis' body only intensified as Elvis became a star. The Jesse Garon being, the destroyer, started to shoot out TV sets during violent outbursts. He surrounded himself with southern buddies and developed a obsession with guns, becoming increasingly paranoid as his strange, cloistered nightlife was termed decadent and maniacal. The

(true) Elvis spirit took uppers, downers, and painkillers to try to get some kind of relief. The Jesse being was some kind of 'sex maniac,' bragging to his stepmother that he had slept with more than a thousand women. Those women meant nothing to the 'true Elvis,' whose greatest love was his mother Gladys."
(see also CAVE, NICK and PRESLEY, JESSE GARON.)

Farrell, Ann

Ann Farrell was one of the many women who made the claim that she had been secretly married to Elvis. The ceremony was alleged to have taken place in Russellville, Alabama in 1957, and according to the story that she sold to the *National Enquirer*, Elvis only married her because she refused to sleep with him unless he did right by her. When asked to produce documentation. howeverer, Ms. Farrell claimed that all documents had been destroyed.

Feathers, Charlie

Blues legend Charlie Feathers in a 1990 interview came out with one of the most extraordinary stories about Elvis to ever go into print.

"Not too many people know it, but Gladys took a trip to Florida without Vernon and was carryin' on with a colored fellow down there and was pregnant right after. Nope, Vernon ain't his daddy. No sir."

"Vernon ain't his daddy, no sir."

Fike, Lamar

At times bulking up to over 300 pounds, Lamar Fike was the heaviest member of the Memphis Mafia. He was also something of a court jester and the butt for Elvis' Jokes. In the fullness of time, he would, intentionally or not, get back at his former employer by giving Albert Goldman all the dirt for his book *Elvis*. *(see also ELVIS and MEMPHIS MAFIA, THE.)*

Films of Elvis Presley

The complete list in order of release:
   Love Me Tender (20th Century Fox, 1956)
   Loving You (Paramount, 1957)
   Jailhouse Rock (MGM, 1957)
   King Creole (Paramount, 1958)
   G.I. Blues (Paramount, 1960)
   Flaming Star (20th Century Fox, 1960)
   Wild In The Country (20th Century Fox, 1961)
   Blue Hawaii (Paramount, 1961)
   Follow That Dream (United Artists, 1962)

Elvis and Judy Tyler in Jailhouse Rock

Kid Galahad (United Artists 1962)
Girls! Girls! Girls! (Paramount, 1962)
It Happened At The World's Fair (Paramount, 1963)
Fun In Acapulco (Paramount, 1963)
Kissin' Cousins (MGM, 1964)
Viva Las Vegas (MGM, 1964)
Roustabout (Paramount, 1964)
Tickle Me (Allied Artists, 1964)
Girl Happy (MGM, 1965)
Harum Scarum (MGM, 1965)
Paradise—Hawaiian Style (Paramount, 1965)
Frankie And Johnny (United Artists, 1966)
Spinout (MGM, 1966)
Easy Come, Easy Go (Paramount, 1966)
Double Trouble (MGM, 1967)

Clambake (United Artists, 1967)
Stay Away, Joe (MGM, 1968)
Speedway (MGM 1968)
Live A Little, Love A Little (MGM, 1968)
Charro! (National General, 1969)
Change of Habit* (Universal, 1969)
The Trouble With Girls (MGM, 1969)
Elvis: That's The Way It Is (MGM
    documentary, 1970)
Elvis On Tour (MGM documentary, 1972)

* Not available on commercial videocassette.

Find Elvis

Optical Novelty Toys

A "magic wand with glittery music notes, hearts and spangles; if you look *very* closely, you'll see Elvis in the gold lame suit and even the pink Caddy! Fun gift idea!" This toy, directly inspired by "Where's Waldo," is one of the stranger pieces of Elvis merchandise to come on the market. "Find Elvis" is in fact an eight-inch-long lucite tube filled with a thick, clear liquid and a lot of glitter in suspension. Floating amid the glitter is a tiny picture of Elvis and an even tinier picture of his car. The idea is to peer into the tube and try to find them. When these objects first came on the market in the fall of 1992, they were the hot item in hip gift shops. The "Find Elvis" does however, cause a certain wonderment. When Elvis first appeared on the TV sets of America in 1956, who would have thought that 35 years later, we'd be looking for him in a plastic tube full of chemicals?

Mail order from Graceland Gifts, 3734 Elvis Presley Boulevard, Memphis, TN 38116.

Finalator, John

John Finalator was the deputy director of the Bureau of Narcotics and Dangerous Drugs who in 1970, would refuse to give Elvis an honourary agent's badge, and set him off on the course that would eventually lead to the legendary White House meeting with Richard Nixon. *(see also NIXON, RICHARD MIL-HOUSE.)*

First Assembly Church of God

The First Assembly Church of God was the Presley family's church when Elvis was a child. Vernon, Gladys, and the young Elvis first attended the one in Tupelo that was located 206 Adams Street, just a couple of blocks from the house where Elvis was born. Later, when the family relocated to Memphis, they continued to worship within the same Pentacostal denomination. Their Memphis church was at 1085 McLemore.

Fish

Despite having recorded songs like "Crawfish" and "Do The Clam," Elvis hated fish, even catfish, the traditional Southern favourite, to the point that he requested Priscilla to refrain from eating fish when he was around.

Flying Elvi

Elvis clad skydivers.

Quote—Anonymous comment.

"I guess jumping out of a plane for Elvis isn't much different from annoying people at airports for Krishna.,"

The Flying Elvi were originally assembled in 1992 for the movie *Honeymoon In Vegas*. Instead of disbanding after the movie wrapped, they took their act on the road (so to speak) and now appear at airshows and open air events all over the world.

Forty-three billion dollars

The figure of $43,000,000,000 is frequently bandied around as Elvis' gross life-time earnings. It is, however, a highly dubious and seemingly greatly exaggerated figure. RCA, at a point in the mid-eighties, stated that Elvis had earned $4.3 billion from his record sales, and that is possibly where the confusion started. Obviously Elvis continues to earn today. His estate was calculated to be worth round $200 million as of mid 1994.

Fox, Michael J.

According to singer Mojo Nixon, there is no Elvis in Michael J. Fox. *(see also NIXON, MOJO.)*

Fried peanut butter and banana sandwich

This signature sandwich will forever be linked with Elvis, and it has become his major culinary contribution to the pop/folk cuisine of Planet Earth. It is constructed from the following ingredients:

1 ripe banana
2 slices of white bread
3 tablespoons of peanut butter
2 tablespoons butter

The banana is mashed in a bowl, while the bread is lightly toasted. (This pre-toasting is crucial since, without it, the sandwich tends to turn soggy or even disintegrate during the frying stage.) The banana is spread on one piece of toast and the peanut butter is spread on the other. The butter is melted in a pan, and when hot, the two halves of the sandwich are slapped together, fried until golden brown and served.

Bacon is included in some variations of the now legendary sandwich, in which case, the bacon is pre-fried to a crisp and inserted between the peanut butter and mashed banana prior to closure of the sandwich. If desired, the hot fat from the bacon can also be substituted for the butter as the frying medium.

G

Gacy, John Wayne

Among the collection of artworks painted on death row and left behind by convicted mass murderer John Wayne Gacy after his execution in May 1994 was a large portrait of Elvis. The paintings were bought at auction by an anonymous Chicago man who said his intention was to destroy them.

Geller, Larry

Larry Geller was Elvis' hairdresser for about ten years between 1964 and the mid-seventies. Geller was an avid devotee of parapsychology and the occult, and after he and Elvis became friends rather than just employer and employee, he introduced Elvis to numerous books on mysticism, pop philosophy, and metaphysics. In the years just prior to Elvis' death, Colonel Parker grew uneasy about the growing influence that Geller was having on Elvis, and used his grip on the Memphis Mafia to break up the relationship.

Geller has co-authored three books about Elvis: *The Truth About Elvis* (1980), *Elvis' Spiritual Journey* (1983) and *If I Can Dream* (1989).

Giddens, Clarence

Clarence Giddens is remarkable in that he is, so far, the only Afro-American to work as a full-time Elvis impersonator. (Although Eddie Murphy was prone to do Elvis bits both as part of his live shows and during his stint on "Saturday Night Live.") He justifies his chosen vocation with the following statement— "Elvis was a Martin Luther King Jr. in the music field. He did not see music as divided by colour. Elvis took rhythm and blues, that couldn't get much airtime in those days, and opened a lot of doors for black artists. Elvis to me is exciting, dazzling, motivating, and in control."

Reports tend to confirm that Giddens sounds a lot like Elvis, but, as to a physical resemblance—"I'd have to go through one of those things that Michael Jackson went through." *(see also I AM ELVIS.)*

Clarence Giddens can be contacted through Billy Sturgis, P.O. Box 834, Nassawadox, VA 23413.

Godfrey, Arthur

Arthur Godfrey, the star of the hugely successful fifties TV and radio shows, "Arthur Godfrey and Friends" and "Arthur Godfrey's Talent Scouts," had the unique, if dubious honor of being the only big time TV host to turn down Elvis for an appearance on his show. Later, such luminaries as Jackie Gleason, Milton Berle, Steve Allen, Ed Sullivan and Frank Sinatra would fight tooth and nail to book Elvis.

Gold Cadillac

Elvis' legendary gold Cadillac, a 1960 series 75 Sedan Limousine was customized by designer George Barris with ten coats of diamond-dust gold pearl paint. The car is valued at $100,000 and was, a various times, put on touring exhibition by Colonel Parker. It is now on permanent display in the Country Music Hall Of Fame in Nashville. *(see also CADILLAC.)*

Gold Lame Suit

The gold lame suit that Elvis can be seen wearing in publicity shots and on dozens of album covers, including *Elvis' Golden Records – Volume II*, was created in 1957 by Nudies of Hollywood, the famous country music costume designers who had previously made outfits for Hank Williams and Patsy Cline, at a cost of $10,000. Elvis apparently hated wearing the suit, finding it too heavy for stage work.

Gold Record

For $135 (at the time of writing), you too can own a "framed and ready to display" facsimile of an Elvis Presley gold record—the kind that the record company presents to artists after they have sold a half-million copies of an album.

Available from Graceland Gifts 3734 Elvis Presley Blvd., Memphis, TN 38116.

Graceland

The original address was 3764 Highway 51, South Memphis. The highway in front of the house has now been renamed "Elvis Presley Boulevard." Graceland is now open to the public as a permanent museum and is the hub of the Elvis

Presley business empire. It averages some 2,500 visitors a day. The house was built in neo-classical style on a 13.8 acre site in 1939 by Dr. Thomas Moore, who named it after his aunt. Graceland was placed on the Register of Historic Places in November 1991. Elvis talking about Graceland:

Graceland is just 15 miles south of Tupelo. When I first bought the estate and mansion for $100,000 in 1958, it was just like living in the country. There was nothing around my place but a few cotton and sugar plantations. The highway was second class. Now the Tennessee Highway Department has resurfaced the highway that runs in front of my estate because the thousands of tourists constantly roaring past, parking, backing up, and turning around had torn it up.

When the highway was put in top shape, it opened the way for a new flood of traffic and a big land boom. Now we're surrounded by all kinds of things I didn't plan on.

My fans don't embarrass me. They're the greatest. I love 'em. Even when they get a little rough, they're swell kids.

The mansion sits directly in the middle of its 14 acres and things are going crazy around the place. A city block, a 25,000 square-foot shopping centre, has gone up—one of those ultra modern buildings. It has everything from clothing stores to supermarkets, barber shops, and even a record store in it. I'm right happy about the record store.

But the point is it's all increasing the traffic in front of my place, until it's almost like living in New York's Times Square. To the north is a new, tall, white Baptist church. Across the highway, to the west, a real estate operator is advertising lots and modern homes at $17,500 a piece. Tractors and bulldozers are ripping the land apart.

I got a list of good decorating ideas for Graceland. I'm always fixing and repairing around the house. I like to do things first class, too. I had one wall knocked out of the first floor of the house to enlarge the room. Then I got a wonderful idea to make the ceiling of my bedroom all velvet. I like bright colors like orange, red, and yellow. They look right nice.

I'm real proud of my Graceland. I'll never leave. If the invasion of my privacy keeps up, it can he easily remedied. We'll just have a solid string of weeping willows planted along the stone fence around the entire estate. That will at least keep noise down and give us privacy.

I only really feel at home in Memphis, at my own Graceland mansion. It isn't that I don't like Hollywood, but a man feels lonesome for the things that are familiar to him, his friends, and acquaintances. I know I do. That's why I would never live in Hollywood permanently. Hollywood's a lovely city. I've learned to appreciate it more since we moved into a Mediterranean-style villa I rent on a Bel-Air hilltop. It's so quiet up there. The place is all marble columns and statuary, a fine home away from home, but home for me will always spell Memphis and Graceland.

Graceland Gifts

The official Graceland mail order catalogue. It is issued four times a year and runs to some sixteen pages.

Write Graceland Gifts, 3734 Elvis Presley Boulevard, Memphis, TN 38116.

Graffiti

The following are examples of graffiti left on the stone wall that surrounds Graceland:

"We lost a King but heaven gained one."
"Elvis is undead!"
"Elvis, the world needs you."
"Elvis, no matter where you go, there you are."
"Elvis, if you read this I know you are alive."
"Elvis, I'm having your baby. 29 Sept '91."
"Fight the power, Elvis was a hero to most."
"Hi Elvis, from Stonehenge."
"Every mountain I have to climb, Elvis carried me over on his back."
"I'm hooked on Elvis. What did I do before I discovered him?"
"Elvis is God."
"Elvis, your spirit lit my way."
"Loving you makes a lonely street a lot easier."
"Elvis, thank you for being our guiding light."
"I heard the call, I made the pilgrimage, I came to Graceland."
"Elvis, you came, you saw, you conquered, you croaked."
"Elvis, the values you tried to hold on to shall live on."
"Elvis saves."
"Elvis, I feel you're here."
"Elvis, can I use your bathroom?"

"Elvis, you caught me in your trap."
"He touched me and now I am no longer the same."
"Thanks for making our honeymoon so special."
"He traveled from Germany to be near you."
"Wanted to be here before I died. I made it."

Some of the writing even stretches to poetry...
"Coming back from Lubbock.
I thought I saw Jesus on the plane,
But it might have been Elvis,
They look kinda the same."

Grenada

Long before the U.S. Postal Service got in on the act, the tiny Caribbean island of Grenada was, in 1979, the first nation to issue an Elvis postage stamp. The United States invaded Grenada in 1983, although the two events are apparently unrelated.

Guitars

In January 1946, for Elvis' eleventh birthday, his mother took him to the Tupelo Hardware Company on Main Street in Tupelo, where she bought him his first guitar for $7.75. Elvis had apparently been lobbying for some time to get a .22 rifle for his birthday, but Gladys had decided that a guitar would be a less dangerous gift. When Elvis discovered that he wasn't going to get the gun on which he'd set his heart, he seemingly threw a temper tantrum right there in the store and it took all the persuasion that Gladys and store proprietor Forest Bobo could muster to get him to accept the guitar as a substitute.

Two guitars figured prominently during the early years of Elvis' career and they were both acoustic. First was the Martin D-28 and then the Gibson J-200. Elvis' original Martin now resides on display in the Country Music Hall Of Fame in Nashville.

After his return from the army, when the guitar became little more than a comfortable prop for Elvis, first in the movies and later in live stage shows, he was pictured playing just about every guitar under the sun. His favourites, however, does seem to have been Gibsons of various kinds, both hollow and solid bodied electric, and when he felt the need to play an acoustic guitar, he would return again and again to the classic J-200.

The fifties saw the marketing of a number of plastic, yet supposedly playable Elvis Presley guitars, although most came with only four strings and how you were supposed to tune the thing was kinda debatable. As objects, however, they were unsurpassed as pieces of flashy fifties kitsch. Most were two-tone, with contrasting inset panels and bore a picture of Elvis, his signature, or both. One model featured a Fender-style cutaway body and another had a mechanical device attached to the neck called "a Hold-A-Chord" that made it possible to form a simple chord by pressing down on a single button and, in theory, one could strum a basic rock tune after just a few minutes practice.

Despite their garishness, the plastic guitars of the fifties were infinitely preferable to today's Elvis souvenir guitar, which is nothing more than a cheap scaled down wooden acoustic flat-top with the words "Sincerely Elvis Presley" inscribed on the body.

As Gibson J-200s can still be purchased today, the Elvis plastic guitars are serious collectors' items.

Guns

Elvis was a gun freak, owning at the time of his death, a collection of some thirty-seven rifles, shotguns, pistols and machine guns. He frequently went around armed, even while at home at Graceland or in Bel Air. At times during the seventies, he would even go on stage with a two-shot derringer strapped to his right ankle.

According to most accounts, Elvis was far from being either a careful or responsible gun owner. During temper tantrums, or on a mere whim, he was prone to whip out a piece and blaze away at all types of inanimate objects including television sets, a summerhouse at Graceland, a chandelier, and a malfunctioning lightswitch in a Las Vegas hotel suite. He also pumped a dozen bullets into the engine and bodywork of a Ferrari that refused to start, and shot holes in the ceiling of a Memphis restaurant when the service wasn't up to his satisfaction. Needless to say, no one ever called the cops on Elvis after any of these episodes. During these various armed freakouts, he narrowly avoided killing or injuring his father Vernon and girlfriend Linda Thompson. Dr. George Nichopoulos was less lucky, being hit in the chest by a spent .22 slug, but fortunately sustaining no major injuries during a TV shooting incident.

Elvis bought a lot of his guns at Kerr's, a sporting goods store in Beverly Hills. In December 1970 alone, Elvis spent $38,000 on various firearms, presumably as Christmas gifts for himself and his henchmen. His purchases included a $19,000 .357 Colt Python.

A customised Colt .45 automatic that had belonged to Elvis with ivory grips inlaid with the TCB lightning flash was sold at Sotheby's in 1994 for $12,000. *(see also SWING SET.)*

Harris, Zelda

Zelda Harris made the claim that she was Elvis' first wife. Her story is that she met Elvis in Mobile, Alabama in 1960 and the two of them were married within twenty-four hours. Like so many of the women who allege that Elvis was their husband, Ms. Harris was unable to produce any conclusive documentation This did not, however, stop the tabloid *The Globe* from running her story in March 1981.

Hart, Cheryl

The story of Cheryl Hartz is one of the great heartstring-twanging, weepy footnotes to the Elvis Legend. Eleven-year-old Cheryl was dying of plastic anemia in a Schnectady New York Hospital, and all she wanted was a signed picture of Elvis. When Elvis heard about this, he immediately airmailed the picture. Cheryl briefly rallied after she received the gift, but died two weeks later.

Hart, Dolores

Dolores Hart (real name Dolores Hicks) co-starred with Elvis as the "good girl" in the movies *Loving You* and *King Creole*. She also dated Elvis for a brief period. In 1963, Hart left the movies and became a nun. Today she is Mother Superior at the Covent of Regina Laudis in Bethlehem, Connecticut. Needless to say, both tabloid writers and fans had a field day with the fact that Hart's conversion was the result of unrequited love for Elvis.

Harum Scarum

Feature film, 1965. Elvis Presley, Mary Ann Mobley, Fran Jeffries, Michael Ansara, Jay Novello, Billy Barty. Directed by Gene Nelson.

Generally acknowledged as the very worst Elvis movie.

Available on videocassette.

Heartbreak Hotel (single)

Single: "Heartbreak Hotel/I Was The One," first released January 1956, RCA G2WB 0209. Elvis Presley (vocals), Scotty Moore & Chet Atkins (guitars), Floyd Kramer (piano), Bill Black (bass), D.J. Fontana (drums), Gordon Stoker, Ben and Brock Speer (backing vocals).

If "Heartbreak Hotel" isn't the greatest rock & roll single of all time, it is certainly the masterwork of rock's formative period.

Heartbreak Hotel (movie)

Feature movie, 1988. David Keith, Tuesday Weld, Charlie Schlatter, Jacque Lynn Colson, Angela Goethals. Directed by Chris Columbus.

Set in 1972, this movie tells the highly whimsical and wholly fictional story of an Ohio teen (Schlatter) just getting his first rock band together, who kidnaps Elvis (Keith) and takes him home to cheer up his divorced mother (Weld). *Heartbreak Hotel* is far from being a truly great movie, but it has its moments, most of which are David Keith doing a creditable Elvis (even if it is Elvis considered as a fantasy figure akin to Santa Claus).

Available on videocassette.

Heartbreak Hotel (plate)

Commemorative plate, 1993.

One of the series of Bradford Exchange mail order plates that possibly deserves an individual note. Certainly, at the time of writing, it was by far the most interesting of the series. Painted in somber sunset tones by Nate Giorgio, it depicts an equally sombre looking Elvis standing outside a run-down flophouse with a sign that reads "Heartbreak Hotel." A second, ghostly image of Elvis looks broodingly down from the sky. Of all of the mass-produced "Elvis icons," this is one of the few that manages to catch the anguish and repressed violence of the music it is supposed to illustrate. *(see also PLATES and ELVIS THE KING.)*

The *Heartbreak Hotel* plate has not been advertised either in the press or on TV for some time, but the Bradford Exchange can be contacted at 1-800-541-8811.

Horrocks, Frankie

Known as "The Button Lady" around Memphis, Frankie Horrocks is an institution. Horrocks, who appears in the documentary movie *Mondo Elvis*, has a story that is both weird and at times, horrific. In 1966, she saw the movie *Blue Hawaii* and "fell in love." She told her husband that she wanted a divorce. After a while, the husband decided he had no choice. The second complaint on the divorce petition was "excessive devotion to Elvis Presley."

For a while, Horrocks and her youngest daughter lived together "like soulmates," devoting their lives to Elvis. Then the daughter was murdered by a psychopath who was subsequently released from jail and killed again. Frankie Horrocks buried her daughter with a copy of the single "Burning Love" in the coffin.

When Elvis died, Horrocks moved to Memphis and has remained there ever since becoming a familiar figure around the city.

In *Mondo Elvis*, she makes a earthily-telling insight into the seeming prudery of a lot of Elvis fans. "Any normal, red-blooded American woman who loves him is a liar if she said, 'I would not want to go to bed with Elvis Presley.' No, I take that back. I met a woman who said if she was given the opportunity of making love to Elvis or having him sing to her, she would want him to sing to her. And I looked at her and I said, 'You're sick.' Personally. I'd want him to sing while he was making love." *(see also MONDO ELVIS.)*

Howard, Edwin

In the mid-fifties, Edwin Howard wrote an entertainment column for the *Memphis Press-Scimitar* titled "Front Row." On 28 July 1954, his column featured a picture of Elvis under the headline "Overnight Sensation." It was the first time that Elvis had ever been written about in the press.

An original copy of this article in good condition would now be priceless.

I am and I was

Reportedly, at a number of shows on what was to be his final 1977 concert tour, Elvis repeated the phrase, "I am and I was," in a low voice that could only be heard by the front rows of the audience. Since that time, fans have invested the words with deep—although, at times, conflicting—mystic or religious significance.

I Am Elvis

A Guide To Elvis Impersonators. Trade paperback book, 1991. By American Graphic Systems: Pocket Books.

This collection of the promotional material and publicity photographs of sixty professional Elvis impersonators would seem to indicate that you don't have to be insane to take the gig, but it sure as hell must help. Included in the book are some slightly bizarre individuals like Clarence Giddens, the black Elvis; Janice Kucera, the female Elvis; Bruce Borders, who divides his time between impersonating Elvis and holding office as mayor of Jasonville, Indiana; and Miguel Quintana who, having been born 19 July 1986, started his career as an Elvis imitator at the age of three, giving him the justifiable claim to having been the youngest Elvis impersonator to date.

I Am Elvis essentially presents the bare facts and offers no commentary or judgment and certainly attempts no insight as to why so many people should have the desire to get up on a stage costumed as Elvis Presley or why the public at large should continue to demonstrate an overwhelming need for these Elvis surrogates. *(see also GIDDENS, CLARENCE and KUCERA, JANICE.)*

Available in bookstores.

India

After the U.S. and Europe, the subcontinent of India was one of the biggest markets for Elvis' movies. In many respects, the worst aspects of Elvis' all-singing, all-dancing, '60s Hollywood films fitted in well with the lavish but equally mindless products of the domestic Indian cinema. The advertising material used in the Indian releases of Elvis' films showed a decidedly swarthy depiction of the star, as did many of the locally produced Elvis souvenirs, a feature that had made them strangely attractive to a certain perverse group of European and American collectors. *(see also BUSTS.)*

I never knew a guitar player who was worth a damn

Thus spake Vernon Presley at the time in the early fifties when Elvis was contemplating a full time career in music. Later, Elvis would have the words engraved on a plaque that he kept hanging in Graceland. *(see also PRESLEY, VERNON.)*

Insomnia

All through his life, Elvis had trouble sleeping. Guitarist Scotty Moore has often recounted how, during the early days on the road when Elvis was first signed to Sun Records, he would remain so hyper after a show that it was frequently necessary for Moore and bass player Bill Black to have to literally walk Elvis around the streets to tire him out so he would be able to get some sleep before getting up to travel to the next gig. Whether this was an indication that, even in the mid-1950s, Elvis was already hitting the diet pills or some other form of uppers or whether he actually suffered from some kind of chronic sleep disorder is a question that will probably never he answered. Certainly in later life, Elvis had many sleep-related problems that were at least partially responsible for the massive drug intake that would eventually kill him.

Internal Revenue Service

At the time of his death, the IRS claimed that Elvis owed them some $10 million dollars in back taxes. Elvis' tax situation was always a mess. The Colonel took no part in the preparation of Elvis' tax returns, and unlike the managers of most major stars, never advised his client regarding investments or tax shelters, always telling him to keep quiet and pay the full amount. The reason for this seems to have been that Parker was nervous that any government scrutiny of Elvis' finances might have revealed his own illegal alien background. In the later years, the responsibilities for taking care of Elvis' taxes fell to Vernon Presley who seemingly was quite out of his depth, and even had difficulty understanding the basic forms. Such was the nature of Elvis business organization and hence the massive debt to the IRS.

International Folklore Review

In one of its 1984 issues, *International Folklore Review* ran an article by Sue Bridwell Beckham that drew religious parallels between the Elvis Legend and Jesus Christ.

"At the mythic age of thirty-three, the age at which Jesus was tried, crucified, and rose from the dead, Elvis taped a concert in front of a live audience that would be aired via satellite around the world. Thus Elvis arose. The television concert was hailed as a revival and even as a 'resurrection.' It paved the way for his first public appearance in nearly a decade in Las Vegas, and for continual live concerts at a spirit-breaking pace until his death in 1977. Thus he became again a "living" musical guru who had flesh and blood contact with his followers. But it would take his death to bring about the transfiguration."

Is Elvis alive? (question)

The ultimate question.

The answer in a nutshell, would seem to be an unequivocal no. This has not, however, stopped a large number of individuals, organisations, book and magazine publishers, and TV producers from building what has, at times, amounted to an entire industry on the idea that, one way or another, Elvis faked his own death and is alive today and living in seclusion.

After the death of any public figure, there seems to be a period of mass rejection when rumours start flying around that maybe the individual in question is not dead after all, but somehow in hiding, in a hospital, in a mental institution. or in some other kind of secret retreat. It happened with Adolf Hitler, James Dean, Buddy Holly, and Jim Morrison and it was virtually inevitable that the same should happen with Elvis. Few would have predicted, however, the extremes to which the stories about Elvis would be taken.

Initially the rumours were confined to a handful of the craziest fans. The first commercial cash-in on the idea that Elvis might have faked his own death came with the publication of *Orion*, Gayle Brewer-Giorgio's fictional account of an Elvis-like rock star who arranged his own death to find peace and freedom from the pressures of fame, and the recordings credited to the singer named Orion that followed. The novel was not a success and Brewer-Giorgio had to wait until 1988 until she really hit paydirt in the Elvis rumour business.

In 1981, a book by Steven C. Chanzes was published that claimed Elvis was not dead and the body intered at Graceland was that of a terminally-ill Elvis look-a-like. Chanzes went on to assert that Charlie Hodge was the Memphis Mafia insider who actually arranged the phony death. Hodge immediately sued both Chanzes and the tabloid, *The Globe*, that serialized his book, for a million bucks. For the moment, that seemed to be the end of the matter and Elvis

should, henceforth rest in peace.

More than Charlie Hodge's lawsuit, in retrospect, it seems that in 1981, the world wasn't quite ready to believe that Elvis was still alive. By far, the majority of fans were still too busy dealing with their shock and grief to want to make the leap into the eerie twilight zone of conspiracy theories and substituted corpses. Seven years later, things had radically changed. By 1988, it seemed that both the world and the media were ready for any kind of craziness. The second book with the title *Is Elvis Alive?* was published and the world went insane.

Although the book is a rambling and occasionally unintelligible catalogue of so-called proofs, underlayed with Brewer-Giorgio's hardly concealed bitterness that her novel *Orion* was a commercial failure, it seemed to hit some strange nerve and the idea that Elvis might be still alive was everywhere.

The main claim to authenticity wasn't so much anything that Brewer-Giorgio might have written, though. It was the audio cassette marketed along with the book. This purported to be a 1981 recording of Elvis talking on the phone, four years after his death. Brewer-Giorgio claimed that the tape had

been given to her by two unidentified women who were apparently in on the secret. The tape was even checked by a well known voice analyst, L.H. Williams, who concluded that the voice was actually Elvis. At the height of the promotion of *Is Elvis Alive?*, a series of TV commercial spots offered potential buyers the chance to dial an 800 number and decide for themselves whether or not it was Elvis.

Subsequently, a more detailed investigation revealed that the tape was in fact a fake. It had been recorded by an Elvis imitator called David Darlock for Stephen Chanzes' *Is Elvis Alive?*. After that project crashed and burned, an edited version of the tape was made available to Tudor Press to be packaged with the Brewer-Giorgio book.

Despite the major doubts cast on Brewer-Giorgio's credibility, she was able to produce a second book and two syndicated TV specials, all seeking to prove that Elvis was still alive.

Even more surprising was the way in which the public seemed to go along with the idea. Almost in the manner of UFOs or bigfoot, Elvis "sightings" started to be reported all over the country. One of the first took place in a Burger King in Kalamazoo, Michigan. Another claim was that Elvis was working for the New York Police apartment under the name of Alvis Lishkowitz. At the most extreme, Elvis was rumoured to have been seen in Chernobyl shortly after the nuclear disaster.

Photographs also started to appear. The 4 October 1988 issue of the *National Examiner* ran a series of photos of a portly sideburned individual alleged to be Elvis walking across a parking lot in Las Vegas. In the same year, an out-of-focus shot of an Elvis-like figure in the poolhouse at Graceland was presented both as evidence that Elvis was alive and also as an actual photo of Elvis' ghost. Memphis Mafia honcho Joe Esposito would eventually go on "Larry King Live" and discredit this picture, stating that the person in the shot was, in fact, Graceland employee Al Strada.

Although the "Is Elvis Alive?" furor had all the elements of both fraud and farce, the way in which it caught the public imagination would seem to be a major symptom of the quasi-supernatural aura that has grown up around Elvis since his death.

(see also BREWER-GIORGIO, GAYLE; DEATH OF ELVIS, THE; and ORION)

Is Elvis Alive? (Chanzes book)

Book, 1981. By Steven C. Chanzes, publisher unknown.

See above. This book is long out of print and copies are virtually impossible to locate.

Is Elvis Alive? (Brewer-Giorgio book)

Paperback book with accompanying audio cassette, 1988. By Gayle Brewer-Giorgio: Tudor Publishing Company.

The second book to use the title. This one came with the infamous telephone cassette that purported to be the core proof that Elvis was alive. Although the book reportedly sold millions, it may well have been massively overprinted, since copies both with and without the tape appear regularly in cutout bins and discount stores.

Jailhouse Rock

Arguably the best of Elvis' musical movie vehicles, if for no other reason that in Vince Everett, Elvis plays about the only thoroughly unlikable character in his entire movie career. (Vince was only redeemed at the end of the movie by a punch in the throat from Mickey Shaughnessy.) This is not to mention the actual "Jailhouse Rock" performance sequence that, in its own way, and despite the Ray Anthony-style brass and voices dubbed onto the movie version of the song, is one of the greatest pieces of rock & roll ever committed to the screen.

According to legend, Elvis refused to ever watch *Jailhouse Rock* following the 1957 auto-wreck death of co-star Judy Tyler.

For a short time in the early nineties, the Turner Broadcast System aired a colourised print of the originally black & white movie in which Elvis, famous in the fifties for his wardrobe of black and shocking pink, appeared to be dressed in discreet shades of brown and green. Mercifully, the colourised print vanished from TV screens in 1993 when it was replaced by a crisp, digitally cleaned up black and white version in letterbox format.

Jailhouse Rock is available as a commercial videocassette.

James Dean Story, The

After the completion of *Love Me Tender* in 1956, producer David Weisbart was contemplating a version of *The James Dean Story* as his next project. Elvis is reputed to have moved heaven and earth to be allowed to play Dean, who was back in those days, along with Marlon Brando, one of Elvis' movie idols and role models as an actor. He apparently even made an offer to Weisbart to completely finance the film. Eventually Weisbart dropped the idea, and the only film of that title was a documentary made by George W. George and Robert Altman of such poor quality that it was withdrawn shortly after its release.

Jeans

Apart from in the movies, Elvis rarely wore jeans. Seemingly, blue jeans and dungarees were too closely associated in Elvis' mind with the poverty of his childhood, when he had no option but to dress in jeans or overalls. Unlike a

Jailhouse Rock

later generation of more middle-class rockers like Bob Dylan and Bruce Springsteen who would even come on-stage in ripped and faded jeans, Elvis saw denim as the work clothes of poor folks and he invariably wore tailored slacks.

Jones, Jim

People's Temple cult leader Jim Jones who, in 1978, killed himself along with 917 of his followers in their Jonestown jungle commune in Guyana, based much of his flamboyant style—particularly a taste for sideburns, medallions, white suits, and mirrored aviator shades—on Elvis.

Jones, Tom

The story persists that the Welsh singer was, in a large part responsible for Elvis deciding to play Las Vegas in the wake of his 1968 TV comeback. At the time, Jones was the new sensation and serious competition to even Frank Sinatra. Insiders claim that Elvis regarded Jones and his hip-shaking stage moves a direct rip-off of his own act, and was determined to beat the Welshman on his own turf.

Later, it seems to have been decided that, since Elvis and Jones enjoyed the loyalty of many of the same fans, it would seem to make more sense for them to be seen as buddies rather than feuding rivals. Reports were circulated of a growing friendship (as far as Elvis' extraordinary lifestyle would allow him to maintain any kind of friendship) and photos were released to the press of Tom Jones and Elvis together in the music room at Graceland.

Juanico, June

Elvis dated June Juanico on a regular basis through the summer of 1956, and the couple was seen together to such an extent that a New Orleans radio station reported that they were engaged to be married. Like so many of the women in Elvis' life, she—and her relationship with Elvis—fell victim to the quantum pressures of his career, and also the machinations of Tom Parker, who until the mid-sixties, feared that to have Elvis' name constantly linked with that of any particular woman would alienate his female fans.

The story of June Juanico's relationship with

From Last Train To Memphis *by Peter Guralnick: Little, Brown.*

Elvis is recounted at length in Peter Guralnick's 1994 book *Last Train To Memphis*. *(see also LAST TRAIN TO MEMPHIS.)*

King Creole

Although hardly a movie classic in its own right, *King Creole* was one of Elvis' markedly better Hollywood efforts, even though the music is a trifle odd, being a unfortunate blend of rock and Dixieland. Similar problems also applied to the story. The original Harold Robbins novel, *Stone For Danny Fisher*, was about corruption in professional boxing. When the central character was made a singer rather than an up-and-coming middleweight contender to accommodate Elvis, the concept of gangsters fighting over who was going to manage him made less-than-perfect sense.

King Creole did, however, have about the most prestigious cast of any Elvis movie, including Walter Matthau as the heavy, Vic Morrow as a punk and Carolyn Jones (who would go on to play Morticia in the TV version of "The Addams Family") as the bad girl.

In some areas of the U.S., *King Creole* was first released as part of a double feature with a western titled *Bullwhip* starring Guy Madison, and Rhonda Fleming. In others it was coupled with the monster movie *Colossus Of New York*.

King Creole is available on commercial videocassette.

King Does The King's Thing

Album, 1969. Stax STS 2015—Albert King.

This 1969 Elvis tribute by legendary bluesman Albert King is just about the only collection of Elvis material played (brilliantly, I might add) in a hard driving R&B style. Tracks include "Don't Be Cruel," "Blue Suede Shoes," "Hound Dog," "Jailhouse Rock" and "Heartbreak Hotel."

Now only available in specialist blues collector stores. but well worth the search.

Kirsch, Jack

Jack Kirsch was the pharmacist at the Prescription House at 1247 Madison Avenue in Memphis who filled Dr. George Nichopoulos' prescriptions for Elvis. Kirsch supplied Elvis with 5,684 pills of various kinds in a single seven month period. He lost his pharmacist's license in May 1980. *(see also DRUGS and NICHOPOULOS, DR. GEORGE C.)*

Kucera, Janice

Born 15 December 1950, Janice Kucera from Exeter, Nebraska, is one of the few women who makes a living imitating Elvis Presley. Originally an Elvis fan of the more conventional kind, she set out for Memphis at the tender age of sixteen in the hope of a close encounter with the King, and did in fact manage to get herself invited to one of Elvis' all night movie parties as the old Memphian Theatre. Three years later, she followed Elvis to Las Vegas and then on to Los Angeles where she managed to land herself a number of minor movie roles.

Devastated by the King's death in 1977, Kucera returned to Exeter, but set out the following year to put her Elvis "interpretation" on the road. Kucera also claims to have had a supernatural visitation from Elvis since his death. "I'd just been on the phone with Elvis' uncle Vester and I was sitting at the kitchen table while Mama was cooking supper when I noticed that there was a man looking in the south kitchen window—and it was Elvis' image! It was his forehead, cheekbones and nose on the window screen. The next day, I went outside and all the limbs on the evergreen tree behind the window were all scorched and singed. The image stayed on the screen for four years before it faded and vanished." *(see also I AM ELVIS and SIGHTINGS.)*

Janice Kucera can be contacted at P.O. Box 345, Exeter, NE 68351.

lang, k.d.

Neo-country singer k.d. lang (the lack of capitalization is her own idea, much in the manner of poet e.e. cummings) has been hailed by the critics and also Madonna as the Elvis of the nineties.

Lansky Brothers

Bernard and Guy Lansky owned the clothing store that bore their name at 126 Beale Street in Memphis where Elvis purchased many of the flamboyant outfits in which he was photographed during his wild days in the fifties. By far, the majority of Lansky's patrons were black, including recording artists like Rufus Thomas and Junior Parker, and also some of Memphis's leading pimps.

By way of a final tribute, the Lansky brothers also supplied the suits for the pallbearers at Elvis' funeral.

Last photograph

The final and somewhat ghoulish photograph of Elvis in his coffin was secretly snapped by Elvis' cousin Bobby Mann and sold to the *National Enquirer* for an undisclosed sum. It ran on the cover of the tabloid on 6 September 1977, and is also featured on the bootleg album *Elvis' Greatest Shit!*

Many friends of Elvis continue to maintain that, from the way the corpse's hair is arranged, the picture is a phony. *(see also ELVIS' GREATEST SHIT!)*

Last Temptation of Elvis, The

Record, double CD set by various artists, 1990.

The *Last Temptation of Elvis* was produced by the British weekly music paper, *New Musical Express,* as a charity fund-raiser for The Nordoff Robbins Musical Therapy Centre in London where music is used as a means of communication and therapy for children who are autistic, psychotic, or have suffered severe brain injuries. The album features twenty-six songs from Elvis' movies and the performers featured on the record range from Bruce Springsteen performing "Viva Las Vegas" and a Paul McCartney version of "It's Now Or

Never" to Robert Plant singing "Let's Have A Party," Aaron Neville's "Young And Beautiful," and the Pogues doing "Got A Lot O' Livin" To Do." Other artists include Hall & Oates, The Cramps, Dion DiMucci, The Jeff Healey Band, and Lemmy from Motorhead. Also included is a previously unreleased version of Elvis himself doing "King Of The Whole Wide World."

The record is a U.K. release available in the U.S. from import record stores: NME CD 038/039.

Last Train to Memphis

Hardback book, 1994. By Peter Guralnick: Little, Brown.

Subtitled "The Rise Of Elvis," *Last Train To Memphis* is a highly detailed —at times almost too detailed—account by respected music critic Peter Guralnick of Elvis' life from his birth in 1935 to 1958 when he was inducted into the Army. According to the publisher's blurb, Guralnick had spent almost a decade researching this book, and it would certainly seem that he had talked to almost all the surviving individuals who were around during Elvis' rise to fame. At times, it provides a virtual day-by-day narrative of Elvis' early years, which although an invaluable historical exercise in getting the story onto paper before memories are totally clouded out by legend, creates moments when the book approaches overkill, telling the reader almost more than he or she wants to know.

Available in bookstores.

Last will and testament

After his death, copies of Elvis' will were being sold around Memphis at four bucks a pop.

Last words

(see OKAY, I WON'T)

Lektronic

The brand of electric razor favoured by Elvis. One reposes on display in the Elvis Presley Museum in Memphis.

Lewis, Jerry Lee

Jerry Lee Lewis, the primal rock & roll madman with a seemingly infinite capacity for drink, drugs, cocktail waitresses, and underaged brides was both blessed and cursed by a highly ambiguous relationship with Elvis Presley. On one hand, he would boast about his lifelong friendship with Elvis, and on the other, it was evident that Elvis' success made Jerry Lee insanely jealous.

State of Tennessee, }
SHELBY COUNTY }

I, B. J. DUNAVANT, Clerk of the Probate Court of this County, do hereby certify that the f…

Thirteen (13) - - - - - - - - - - - - - - ….pages contain a full, true and exact cop…

Last Will and Testament of Elvis A. Presley, Deceased·

as the same appears of record or on file in Will Book 209, Page 266

of this office.

IN TESTIMONY WHEREOF, I ha·e hereunto set my hand and affixed the seal of said Court, …

in the City of Memphis this 24th day of August 19 77.

B. J. DUNAVANT. Clerk

By Margaret Hare

Copy of Elvis' will

Both Elvis and Jerry Lee started out together at Sun Records, and for a while in the late fifties, it seemed as though Jerry Lee might be a serious rival to Elvis. Then Lewis' career became bogged down in the scandal of his bigamous marriage to underage Myra Gayle, and Elvis proved unstoppable.

In the mid-seventies, a crazy, drunk Jerry Lee crashed his car into the gates of Graceland, waving a gun and screaming that Elvis should come out and talk to him. Later, Jerry Lee would claim that he wanted to talk to Elvis about his

Collage by Dave Abramson, 1988

drug habit, feeling that if he could bring Elvis home to rock & roll, the man's life could be saved. Jerry Lee was of course, the cousin of later-to-be-disgraced TV preacher Jimmy Swaggart, and familiar with the forcible redemption of sinners.

Jerry Lee was also well aware of the drugs that Elvis was taking. Both men were patients of Dr. George Nichopoulos and although the prescriptions written for Jerry Lee were smaller than ones that went to Graceland, it wasn't by much.

When Jerry Lee hit hard times just after Elvis' death, he wasn't above going along with a piece of Elvis-orientated recording trickery. The idea of the album *Duets* (Sun 1011) by "Jerry Lee Lewis and Friends" was to con the public into believing that Elvis was the other unnamed singer. In fact, the Elvis-sounding vocals were by Charlie Rich and Jimmy Ellis. Ellis would later become part of the Orion deception. *(see also MILLION DOLLAR QUARTET and ORION.)*

A biography of Jerry Lee Lewis by Nick Tosches titled *Hellfire* is one of the all-time finest pieces of writing about rock & roll. The book has long been out of print, but can occasionally be found in stores that specialize in books about music.

License plates

A number of Elvis automobile license plates are currently on the market. They include one in white on black that reads "ELVIS" and in smaller type, "That's Rock-N-Roll"; a replica of a Tennessee license plate with the number "1-ELVIS"; and a full-colour plate that bears the words "Elvis, The Sun Never Sets On A Legend." Obviously these are not legal license plates and can only be used as home or garage decorations or displayed on cars registered in states that don't require drivers to display a front license plate.

Available in souvenir stores.

Lichter, Paul

Paul Lichter is a longtime fan and collector of Elvis memorabilia. He now runs a mail order operation that he proudly proclaims is "licensed by Graceland."

Paul Lichter can be contacted at 1-800-ELVIS-68

Life and Cuisine of Elvis Presley, The

Hardback books, by David Adler: Crown.

Another of the many Elvis cookbooks that flooded the market in the early nineties. This one aims for a full measure of decidedly sick humour, including as it does a section titled "Love Me Slender – The Elvis Diets" (amphetamines washed down with a Diet Shasta was a staple.)

Available in bookstores.

Listening to Elvis

Song, 1985.

We got into a fight when Elvis died . . .
We ran out to some bar in town
Some big mouth drunk was makin' jokes
Putting Elvis down
My baby gave him fair warnin'
Everybody said
But when he sang "Don't Be Cruel"
Baby lost his cool
And shot him dead.
>   (Written by Scott Kempler
>   and sung by Syd Straw.)

Little Enis

Little Enis was an odd, minor legend way out on the mutant fringes of the Elvis Universe. One of the very first Elvis imitators, Little Enis started "doing" Elvis shortly after the release of "Heartbreak Hotel." By all accounts, Enis was a heavy drinker whose shows could degenerate into drunken chaos, with Enis stumbling over tables, fondling women in the audience and generally screwing up. The odd thing was, that despite the excessiveness of his antics, Little Enis was able to maintain a career until his reported death sometime in the seventies.

That a man should devote his entire life attempting to be Elvis Presley was strange enough, but the core joke of his entire career was the strangest of all. Little Enis selected his name on the idea that, if Elvis was Elvis the Pelvis, he was Enis the Penis. More about Enis can be found in Greil Marcus's book *Dead Elvis. (see also DEAD ELVIS.)*

Live ammunition

According to Dennis Hopper, who hung out with Elvis when he first arrived in Hollywood, Elvis had some serious misconceptions regarding how movies were made. One of the most major was that Elvis, prior to the making of *Love Me Tender*, firmly believed that live ammunition was used in the filming of movie gunfights.

Living Colour

In 1990, rock band Living Colour put out the single "Elvis Is Dead" (Epic). The lyrics were as follows:

Tabloids scream
Elvis seen
At a shopping mall
That's the kind of talk
That makes my stomach crawl

Picture a zombie Elvis.
In tacky white jumpsuit
Just imagine a rotting Elvis
Shopping for fresh fruit...

Love Me Tender (candy bar)

A Elvis-related candy bar that came on the market around 1956. These are now extremely rare items and a single bar in its original wrapping is worth around $75 to collectors.

Love Me Tender (song)

The song "Love Me Tender" is in fact a reworking of the traditional tune "Aura Lee" that dates back to the Civil War.

Lubbock, Texas

Great Moment In Rock & Roll History.

On 15 October 1955, two local musicians calling themselves Buddy & Bob opened for Elvis at the Cotton Club dance hall in Lubbock, Texas. The Buddy of the duo would later find fame as Buddy Holly. This was one of few times—possibly the only time—that Elvis appeared on the same stage as another contemporary rock legend. Normally the Colonel kept Elvis well away from other noted rockers like Little Richard or Gene Vincent. He preferred that the opening acts on Elvis Presley stage shows should be lame comics or broken-down Irish tenors. The Colonel's theory was that, after enduring an hour or so of pure boredom, the kids would be ready for anything by the time that Elvis hit the stage.

Mabe, Joni

Elvis-obsessed artist Joni Mabe first came
into the public eye when her painting *A Love
Letter To Elvis* was one of the pieces on show
at an exhibition titled "Elvis The King, A Folk
Hero" at the Primitivo Gallery in San
Francisco. Critic Greil Marcus said of her
work "you couldn't tell the dementia from the
parody, if there was any."

A traveling exhibition of Mabe's work now
tours the world. In July and August of 1994, it
was staged at London's Royal Festival Hall
Gallery. She also manufactures limited edition
Elvis prayer mats.

Joni Mabe, 1983
Love Letter To Elvis

Mafia

Tabloid would-be scandal.

The day after Valentine's day—15 February 1993—the London tabloid
Daily Mirror came out with a full page picture of Elvis and a screaming banner headline "MURDERED BY THE MAFIA." The story that followed, however, proved a great deal more tenuous and less confident. The kernel of truth
in the story was that Vernon Presley, acting on Elvis' behalf, had engaged in an
ill-advised business deal with an individual called Fredick Pro, with regard to
the purchase of Elvis' new private jet, the Convair 800 *Lisa Marie* that was to
replace his older Lockheed JetStar.

After a series of complex transactions, Vernon and ultimately Elvis found
that, in a nutshell, he'd been taken for well over a million bucks. According to
the *Mirror* story, subsequent investigations seemed to indicate that Pro had
mob ties, was under investigation by the FBI and a case was being prepared for
presentation to a grand jury. By that token, it was possible that Elvis or Vernon, as alleged victims, might have been called as witnesses. Before the case
could come to court, however, Elvis died.

At this point, the *Mirror* makes a massive leap of speculation suggesting

WORLD EXCLUSIVE   ELVIS THE SECRET FILES

MURDERED
BY THE
MAFIA

Shocking story that links Mob with his death

IT WAS 2.30pm on 16 August, 1977. As the two paramedics rushed into Graceland they heard an unseen child crying: "My daddy, my daddy . . . I think he's dead."

The bedroom was in chaos. Clothes and papers were strewn everywhere. A Colt .45 gun lay on a bookcase and a syringe close by. In the bathroom, a woman was trying to give mouth-to-mouth resuscitation to the man lying on the floor. He was heavily-built and naked except for a pair of gold pyjama trousers. His skin had turned blue.

The paramedics did their best. But it was hopeless. There was no pulse, no breathing, no blood pressure.

Elvis Presley was dead.

Natural causes, accidental drug overdose, suicide . . . the theories have been endless. There was even one that the rock star's death was faked as part of

an elaborate FBI plot to shield him from the Mafia. But his personal physician voiced another more sinister possibility: Elvis was murdered.

That belief has been lent further weight by best-selling author John Parker.

Parker has delved into 3,000 pages of confidential files to piece together an explosive story. Elvis, he reveals, was the innocent victim in a major FBI criminal investigation. He had also become unwittingly involved with the Mafia And, on the very day he died, evidence from himself and his father was due to be presented to a grand jury in a fraud at the heart of a $2.4 billion phoney-bond scam linked to key Mafia families.

Today the *Daily Mirror* unlocks *Elvis: The Secret Files*, Parker's powerful cocktail of drugs, cover-ups and conspiracy. And the disturbing truths surrounding the death of The King.

● FULL STORY – TURN TO NEXT PAGE

that because Elvis could have been a potential witness, he was actually murdered to ensure his silence (and also to ensure the paper's lurid headline). The paper seems to have totally ignored all the other investigations that concluded his death was an unfortunate result of his massive, but certainly voluntary, consumption of prescription drugs. Such is the way of things in the world of the tabloids.

The whole story appeared to have been gleaned from a book *Elvis: The Secret Files*, that saw the light of publication in the U.K., but never came out in the U.S. *(see also DEATH OF ELVIS, THE.)*

Mailbox

I don't want to offend the most devoted of Elvis fans, but I can only figure that you've gotta be pretty devoted to place an Elvis mailbox outside your house. You'd also have to live in an extremely law-abiding neighbourhood. Around my way, an Elvis mailbox wouldn't last five minutes before it was stolen. Yet one is currently on the market.

Available (by mail) from Graceland Gifts, 3734 Elvis Presley Boulevard, Memphis, TN 38116.

Martin, Dean

Although not usually recognised in most critical analysis of Elvis' musical work, the hard drinking Italian crooner-Rat Packer was one of the young Elvis Presley's favourite singers and Elvis himself cites him as an influence on his emergent ballad-style singing.

Masks

Since way back in the late sixties, joke and magic shops have featured full-head rubber masks of Elvis complete with highly unnatural black rubber hair and sideburns. When they first started appearing they hung beside masks of Richard Nixon and Henry Kissinger. Today, they're next to Bill Clinton and Saddam Hussein. Elvis' mask is by no means the longest seller, however. Masks of both the Frankenstein Monster and the Creature From The Black Lagoon have been around since the fifties.

Some stores also feature cheaper plastic, face-only masks of the kind that are secured by a length of elastic around the back of the head.

It's kind of unfortunate that no one saw fit to make a death mask of Elvis for posterity as was done with Napoleon and Alexander the Great. Oh well.

McDonald's

TV commercial, 1990.

Through 1990, McDonald's ran a series of "nostalgia"-orientated hamburger commercials. In one, set in 1956, two preteen sisters wait with baited breath for Elvis to come on "The Ed Sullivan Show." The family gathers around the black & white fifties TV set. Suddenly, the set goes dead. The girls are devastated. To console them, Dad takes them to the brand new McDonald's "for their first time." A voice-over by one of the now-grown up sisters acknowledges that they may have "missed out on part of rock & roll history. Somehow, that night it didn't seem so matter so much."

As the family leaves the Golden Arches, Mom smiles smugly. "So, wasn't that better than ol' what's his name?" The grown daughter's voice-over returns, "Years later, we found that it wasn't a blackout. Dad had pulled the plug." The voice over didn't add "so we murdered Dad and buried his body in a shallow grave in the yard," although every Elvis-fearing American wished that it had.

McDowell, Ronnie

If the number of times that his voice has been used to substitute for Elvis in films and TV shows made since Elvis' death is any indication, Ronnie McDowell has to be the leading Elvis sound-a-like. McDowell has provided the singing voice for Kurt Russell in the movie *Elvis*, and for Don Johnson in *Elvis and The Beauty Queen*. His other credits include the mini-series "Elvis and Me" and the TV series "Elvis."

In 1977, McDowell cut an Elvis tribute single, "The King Is Gone," which reached number thirteen on the Billboard Hot 100.

Me and Elvis

Me and Elvis
Never worried about the cops
He flashed the badge he got from Nixon
Every time that we got stopped.
(From "Me And Elvis" by Human Radio.)

Mechanical Elvis

This is one of the most delightful Elvis items currently on the market. Of Japanese origin and made from die-cast steel and plastic, when the mechanism is activated, a fairly life-like figure of Elvis makes his moves on a tiny stage set. Described like this, the mechanical Elvis sounds a little silly, but it is so infinitely superior in the craftsmanship and attention to detail in its design and manufacture than so much of the other stuff on the market, particularly the ugly Elvis dolls that are around at the moment, that it deserves an honorable mention. It is, however, expensive.

Available from toy stores, particularly the kind that specialize in clockwork and mechanical toys.

Meditation Gardens

The Meditation Gardens at Graceland where Elvis, his mother, father, and grandmother are all laid to rest, was originally built for Elvis in 1963 by Anne Lacker and Bernie Grenadier. Although it is now the focal point of any visit to Graceland, the fact tends to be forgotten that the garden is by no means Elvis or Gladys Presley's first resting place. Both Elvis and Gladys were originally buried in Forest Hill Cemetery. On the night of 2 October 1977 (a Sunday), both bodies were exhumed and moved to their new graves in Graceland.

According to legend, on the night of Elvis' death, the lights in Meditation Gardens all mysteriously failed.

Memphis Mafia, The

It was only natural that from the moment that he rose to fame, fan hysteria should dictate Elvis travel with an entourage of bodyguards, hangers-on, and retainers. As time progressed, however, the Elvis machine served not only to protect the star, but to completely cut him off from the outside world and outside influences to the point that, at the end of his life, Elvis had become one of the most isolated individuals on the planet.

Originally known as El's Angels or Elvis Presley's boys, The Memphis Mafia came into being during the late fifties, when Elvis felt a strong need for a "down-home" entourage to give him a sense security both in the alien world of Hollywood show business and the total—and sometimes dangerous—insanity of touring.

Through the sixties, following the death of Gladys Presley, the Memphis Mafia ceased to be just traveling companions and took up virtual residence at Graceland, cocooning the star in a macho, and often very juvenile, good ol' boy environment in which he could do no wrong and was refused nothing. This was basically when the trouble started.

Elvis' entourage were not particularly well paid. During the sixties, they averaged around $250 a week. In the seventies, this rose to a $450 average. The fringe benefits were, however, immense. On a whim, Elvis would hand out gifts of cars, jewelry, and cash, and was usually good for loans and the down payments on houses.

The leading members of the Memphis Mafia were—Joe Esposito, Lamar Fike, Jerry Schilling, Alan Fortes, Sonny West, Marty Laker, Charlie Hodge, Red West, Billy Smith, Gene Smith, Ray Sitton, Marvin Gambill, Patsy Gambill, Bitsy Mott, Louis Harris, George Klein, Jimmy Kingsley, and Cliff Gleaves.

Me 'n' Elvis

Book, 1985. By Charlie Hodge with Charles Goodman: Castle Books.
Unremarkable memories of one of the Memphis Mafia.
Out of print.

Meyer, Alan

Ex-NASA engineer Alan Meyer, who works Las Vegas under the name "Alan" is reputed to be the world's highest paid Elvis imitator. He claims to be able to command up to $50,000 a week for his shows.

Midnight Cowboy

One of the great missed chances.

Elvis was initially offered the Jon Voight role of Joe Buck in the John Schlesinger's brilliant study of New York lowlifes. Seemingly Elvis and the Colonel couldn't get past the character's lack of appeal and the brutal realism of the script and see the potential for Elvis as an actor. Even with Elvis' movie career going down in flames by this time (this was the year Elvis made *Charro!* and *The Trouble With Girls*), the Colonel still insisted on playing to the lowest common fan factor. *(see also STAR IS BORN, A; RAINMAKER, THE; and THUNDER ROAD.)*

Million Dollar Quartet, The

Album: Recorded 1956, released 1981.

For many years, this record was treated as though it was the Holy Grail of rock & roll. On 4 December 1956, back in Memphis for the holidays, Elvis dropped by the Sun Records studio, showing off nineteen-year-old Vegas showgirl Marilyn Edwards on his arm. Carl Perkins was in the studio cutting tracks and both Jerry Lee Lewis and Johnny Cash had also dropped by the Sun offices on that particular afternoon. The four musicians fell into an impromptu jam session as Sun boss Sam Phillips rolled tape. With Elvis signed to RCA for more than a year, the legal complications were too great for Phillips to ever release the recordings. The tapes were shelved and forgotten by all but a handful of obsessive fans who seemed to feel they might contain the secrets of the universe.

After Shelby Singleton bought Sun Records in 1969, bootleg excerpts from the tapes started to appear, but it wasn't until 1981, however, that a deal was finalised between Sun, RCA, and the Elvis Presley Estate to put out a legitimate version of the legendary session. As it turned out, the Million Dollar Quartet was something of a musical disappointment, a raucous and disorganised sing-a-long of contemporary hits and a great deal of gospel music.

Available on CD (Sun 1006).

Minstrel, The

Limited edition book, 1976. By Bernard Benson: Minstrel Publishing Company.

This strange, leather-bound artifact originally sold for $250. The brief 1,600 word text and stick figure drawings purported to be a mystic analysis of the Elvis Presley story. It apparently went over big with Elvis and the Memphis Mafia to the point where Charlie Hodge called it "the truest story about Elvis ever written."

Now only available from rare book dealers.

Mondo Elvis

TV/video documentary (first titled *Disciples Of Rock*), 1981. Produced and directed by Thomas Corby: Monticello Productions.

A deliberately bizarre look at the extreme, white trash outer limits of Elvis devotion, including some truly disturbing Elvis imitators and individuals who believe they are in psychic touch with Elvis. The high point of the one-hour show are the Carroll twins, two weird, spooky sisters who look more like Elvis than Lisa Marie and are totally convinced that they are Elvis' secret daughters. *(see also HORROCKS, FRANKIE.)*

Available on videocassette.

Money Fall Out Of The Sky

Song.

> I want to live—like Elvis
> Drive a car—like Elvis
> I wanna sleep—like Elvis
> Walk around—like Elvis
> Take drugs—like Elvis
> Make love—like Elvis
> Go to hell—like Elvis
>> (Lyrics from "Money Fall Out Of The Sky" by the New York post-punk band Cool It, Reba.)

Moore, Scotty

Born Winfield Scott Moore III in 1931, Scotty Moore was Elvis' first guitar player and more responsible for both Elvis' initial sound—and perhaps even Elvis' initial recording success—than is usually recognised. Before teaming up with Elvis, Scotty Moore played with bassist Bill Black in Doug Poindexter's Starlight Ramblers, and in the early days of Elvis' career, when he and Black were known as The Blue Moon Boys, Moore even acted as ad hoc manager.

Moore and Black split with Elvis in late 1957, angry that while Elvis was making millions, the Colonel seemed to be content to pay them a pittance of a couple of hundred bucks a week. Both Black and Moore continued to record with Elvis until he went into the Army. After Elvis' return in 1960, the split with Bill Black became complete while Scotty continued to play guitar on Elvis' records until 1968 and also appear on the NBC TV special.

Oddly, after finishing the TV special, Scotty Moore, although supposedly an old and valued friend, would never see Elvis again.

In 1964, Scotty Moore recorded a solo album *The Guitar That Changed The World*—Epic LN 24103. *(see also BLACK, BILL and BLUE MOON BOYS.)*

Music Boxes

Over the years, a number of Elvis music boxes have been marketed. Since music box mechanisms lend themselves more naturally to slow ballads rather than rock & roll songs, almost all Elvis music boxes over the years have tended to play "Love Me Tender."

The Elvis
You Can Dance To

*I*n riveting artwork...
Playing "Heartbreak Hotel"...
The "'68 Comeback Special"
Music Box

While the older versions are now collectors' items, music boxes currently on the market include a polished wooden box with an enlargement of the Elvis postage stamp inlaid in the lid, a ten-inch high smoked acrylic guitar, and a clear plastic grand piano with a picture of Elvis engraved in the lid that doubles as a jewelry box. A ceramic, snuffbox-sized box, showing Elvis in his leather costume from the 1968 NBC comeback TV special is unusual in that it actually plays "Heartbreak Hotel."

Most of the currently available boxes can be found at novelty and collectors' stores.

Mystery Train

Feature film, 1992. Joe Strummer, Screaming Jay Hawkins. Directed by Jim Jarmusch.

Movie maker Jim Jarmusch's examination of Elvis as supernatural myth takes place in a run-down Memphis hotel, where a portrait of Elvis on black velvet stares down from the wall in every room. The guests include two teenage Japanese Elvis pilgrims, a stranded Italian woman who encounters Elvis' ghost, and three drunken petty criminals who have just robbed and killed a liquor store owner. Although a lot of the movie doesn't work, it does have its moments, most of which are supplied by blues legend Screaming Jay Hawkins who plays the implacable night clerk.

Available on videocassette.

Neutrogena

Elvis' favourite brand of soap.

Newton, Billie Joe

In the 17 March 1981 issue of the weekly tabloid *The Globe*, Ms. Newton claimed that she had been Elvis' first wife and that she bore him three children, giving birth to the first of these at the tender age of nine. She further stated that she was divorced from Elvis in 1956—when she was still only fifteen—at the suggestion of Colonel Tom Parker. Unfortunately, Newton was unable to substantiate any of her claims. Seemingly all records including birth and marriage certificates had been destroyed.

Newton, Wayne

Legendary Las Vegas lounge singer Wayne Newton is in regular psychic contact with Elvis and has seen his ghost on more than one occasion. At least, this is what Newton told the *National Enquirer* in 1987, in a story that ran in the tabloid's 4 August edition of that year under the banner headline "Elvis' Ghost Talks To Me."

Nichopoulos, Dean

In an odd twist of legend, the son of the notorious Dr. Nick claims that he was miraculously healed by Elvis after he had hurt his leg in a skiing accident.

Nichopoulos, Dr. George C.

In the eyes of many Elvis fans, George Nichopoulos—the notorious Dr. Nick—was nothing less than the man who killed Elvis. This judgment may be a little harsh, but certainly he did very little to keep Elvis alive, and for a time after Elvis' death, he had to be closely guarded from attempts on his life by vengeful fans. One actually shot at him at a football game in Memphis in 1979.

Ultimately, Dr. Nick would be acquitted of malpractice and unethical conduct by a jury, but the fact does remain that during the period between 20 January 1977 and Elvis' death on 16 August of that year, Dr. Nick prescribed 5,684 pills, either downers or speed—an average of twenty-five pills a day.

Nipper

Nipper, the RCA victor trademark dog listening to a phonograph appeared on all of Elvis' RCA recordings. The real Nipper was born in Bristol, England in 1884 and died in 1895. After his death, his master, painter Francis Barroud, had him stuffed.

Elvis kept a small statue of Nipper in his bedroom at Graceland.

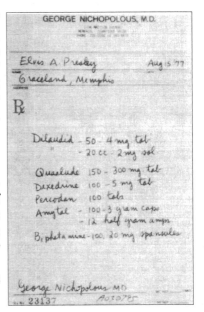

Nixon, Mojo

Cow-punk/psychobilly singer/social commentator Mojo Nixon revealed in the song "Elvis Is Everywhere" that Elvis is indeed everywhere (including the "Bermuda Triangle – Elvis eats boats") except apparently in the soul of actor Michael J. Fox. "Elvis is Everywhere" can be found on the album *Frenzy* (IRS). *(see also FOX, MICHAEL J.)*

Nixon, Richard Milhouse

Elvis wanted to be an example to young people. Some say that because he used drugs, he couldn't. But they overlooked the fact that he never used illegal drugs. The drugs were always prescribed by his physician. He was a very sincere and decent man.
                                                        —Richard M. Nixon

It was 20 December 1970, and Elvis Presley was flying to Washington D.C. on an American Airlines DC-9. In the warm gloom of the first-class cabin, the other passengers were just starting to become accustomed to the fact that the King of Rock & Roll was on the plane. What they didn't know was that Elvis was driven by an obsession. Elvis flagged down a passing cabin attendant and asked her for writing materials. Gripping the ballpoint pen with the airline logo and frowning in concentration, he began a letter to the President of the United States, Richard Nixon.

"Dear Mr. President,

"Let me first introduce myself, I am Elvis Presley and I admire you greatly and have great respect for your office…"

Dear Mr. President.

First I would like to introduce myself. I am Elvis Presley and admire you and Have great Respect for your office. I talked to Vice President Agnew in Palm Springs 3 weeks ago and expressed my concern for our country. The Drug Culture, the Hippie Elements, the SDS, Black Panthers, etc do not consider me as their enemy or as they call it the Establishment. I call it America and I Love it. Sir I can and will be of any Service that I can to help the country out. I have no concern or Motives other than helping the country out. So I wish not to be given a title or an appointed position. I can and will do more good if I were made a Federal agent at Large, and I will help out by doing it my way through my communications with people of all ages. First and Foremost I am an entertainer but all I need is the Federal credentials. I am on this Plane with Sen. George Murphy and We have been discussing the problems that our country is faced with.

So I am Staying at the Washington Hotel Room 505-506-507. I have 2 men who work with me by the name of Jerry Schilling and Sonny West. I am registered under the name of Jon Burrows. I will be here for as long as it takes to get the credentials of a Federal agent. I have done an in depth study of Drug Abuse and Communist Brainwashing Techniques and I am right in the middle of the whole thing, where I can and will do the most good. I am Glad to help just so long as it is kept very Private. You can have your staff or whomever call me anytime today, tonight or tomorrow. I was nominated this coming year one of America's Ten most outstanding young men. That will be in January 18 in my Home Town of Memphis Tenn. I am sending you the short autobiography about myself so you can better understand this approach. I would Love to meet you just to say hello if you're not to Busy.

Respectfully,
Elvis Presley

P.S. I believe that you Sir were one of the Top Ten Outstanding Men of America also.

I have a personal gift for you also which I would like to present to you and you can accept it or I will keep it for you until you can take it.

Mr. Presleys Numbers
These are all my Pvt. numbers.
Beverly Hills 278-3496
278-5935
Palm Springs's 325-3241
Pvt #
Memphis 397-4427
398-4882
398-9722
Pvt #
Col. P.S. # 325-4781
Col. R.H. # 274-8498
Col. off. Mp 870-0270

WASHINGTON HOTEL) PHONE ME 85900
Rm 505-506.
507
UNDER THE NAME
OF JON BURROWS

PRIVATE
AND CONFIDENTIAL

atta. President Nixon
via Sen George Murphy
from
Elvis Presley

Elvis' letter to Nixon

Elvis continued for another five pages in a cramped and none-too-legible hand, explaining how he was willing to play an active part in the war on drugs if only the President would grant him some kind of official status and give him a badge. "The drug culture, the hippie element, the SDS, the Black Panthers do not consider me their enemy...or part of what they call the establishment..." Elvis seemed to be offering to devote his free time to becoming "a Federal drug agent at large." It also seemed that maybe Elvis wasn't thinking too rationally.

In fact, the truth was a little less grandiose and high-minded. What Elvis really wanted was the badge. Elvis collected police badges. It was a habit that he'd almost certainly picked up from the Colonel. Tom Parker was well aware that cozying up to the local cops and getting himself made an honorary deputy sheriff or some such thing made the life of a tour promoter a great deal easier. Elvis, on the other hand, just liked badges—and the one that he didn't have in his collection was that of an agent of the Federal Bureau of Narcotics (later the DEA). Elvis had made requests, but they'd been met with chilly refusal. The Bureau didn't hand out badges to rock stars, no matter how famous. Now it seemed that Elvis was going to the President himself. He was going to attempt a snow job on Nixon.

Arriving in the capital, Elvis decided that the mail didn't cut it. He would go to the White House in person. At around eight in the morning, Elvis' limo arrived at the White House gates. Elvis wanted to hand deliver his note and demanded an immediate audience with the President. He was told that his request would be considered, and after leaving every conceivable phone number at which he might be reached, Elvis went back to his Washington Hotel to wait for the call. The Presley letter might have been consigned to the nut pile except that it was spotted by a bright young Nixon aide named Dwight Chapin. He passed the letter on to White House Chief of Staff and future Watergate conspirator H.R. Haldeman with a memo that pointed out "...it would be wrong to push Presley off onto the Vice President...if the President wants to meet some bright young people, Presley might be the one to start with."

Haldeman went for it, and at 12:45 the same day, 21 December, Elvis Presley was ushered into the oval office. First the photographs were taken, and then Elvis presented the President with a commemorative World War II Colt .45 pistol and seven silver bullets. After the slightly strange gift, Elvis then launched into his pitch about how he was in a unique position to infiltrate the drug culture. According to the official record from the Nixon Archives, Elvis seemed to blame a lot of America's troubles on the Beatles. "'The Beatles have been a real force for anti-American spirit.' (Presley) said that the Beatles came to this country, made their money, and then returned to England where they promoted an anti-American spirit. The President nodded. Presley indicated to Nixon, in a very emotional manner that 'he was on his side.'"

At that point, Elvis made the mistake of attempting to hug Nixon, in the manner of Sammy Davis, Jr. Nixon, the President who couldn't stand to be touched by strangers, started making covert signals to his aides. Give this maniac his badge and get him out of here. Oblivious to the confusion that he'd caused, Elvis became an honorary Federal agent and got his badge. He went home to Graceland to celebrate Christmas and Nixon went back to running the war in Vietnam.

In 1973, Nixon requested that Elvis play at the White House. Traditionally artists perform at the White House for free, but the Colonel demanded a fee of $25,000 for the gig, and refused to back down even in the face of tradition.

Copies of the photographs taken at the Elvis/Nixon meeting can be purchased from the National Archives. *(see also ELVIS UNDERCOVER.)*

O

Elvis' blood type.

Official Elvis Presley Fan Club of Great Britain, Worldwide

Founded in 1956 by Jeannie Seward, the Official Elvis Presley Fan Club Of Great Britain, Worldwide is the world's oldest established Elvis Presley fan club.

Contact the club at P.O. Box 4, Leicester, England.

Okay, I won't

According to Ginger Alden, Elvis' last words were "Okay, I won't," spoken in response to Alden's warning not to fall asleep in the bathroom. A less savoury version of the story claims that Elvis' last words were "Ginger, I'm going for a shit."

1-CF653

The license number of the white Cadillac hearse that carried Elvis' body from Graceland to Forest Hill Cemetery.

Operation Elvis

Hardback book, 1960. By Alan Levy.

Operation Elvis was a quickly produced, journalistic account of Elvis' military career. The British edition was serialised in the *London Daily Mail* just prior to publication.

Long out of print and a very rare item.

Orbison, Roy

Roy Orbison was the one singer in the field of rock & roll who Elvis believed had a voice that seriously challenged his.

Orion

Orion is one of the stranger by-products of the clamour that surrounded the death of Elvis, and the claims that he wasn't really dead. The story starts in 1972, when a singer called Jimmy Ellis went into Sun studios to cut a reprise of Elvis' "That's All Right (Mama)/Blue Moon Of Kentucky." Ellis' voice sounded so much like Elvis that Shelby Singleton, who had bought Sun Records from Sam Phillips, decided to put the single out with a question mark instead of an artist's credit. The idea was to con the fans into believing that this was an alternate take of the original Elvis single.

The scam worked well enough to encourage Singleton to try it again with the Jerry Lee Lewis *Duets* album, which again hinted that Elvis was singing on a number of tracks. If Ellis had any reservations about this unspoken duplicity, he certainly didn't voice them.

In 1979, things took a turn for the deeply weird when Ellis took the identity of Orion Eckely Darnell, the character created by a Marietta, Georgia housewife named Gayle Brewer-Giorgio in her novel *Orion*. Orion Darnell was an Elvis-like rock star who had faked his own death to escape from the pressures of fame. Brewer-Giorgio claimed that she had spontaneously sat down to write the novel on the day that Elvis died, but somewhere along the course of its creation, fiction and reality seemed to become confused. Either Brewer-Giorgio convinced herself that what she was writing was the truth, or she saw the perfect hustle. Whichever it was, she turned proving the theory that Elvis was still alive into a multi-milllon dollar industry, and Jimmy Ellis recorded a number of singles and four albums as Orion, starting with *Reborn* (Sun 1912) in 1979, with Ellis, who was roughly Elvis' build, posing on the cover in a mask.

By 1983, Ellis had had enough of the Orion business. He quit Sun Records and never appeared as Orion again. Even though Ellis publicly repeated that he was Orion, a certain lunatic fringe of Elvis fans refused to believe that this wasn't merely a further phase in the conspiracy, and to this day, there are those who insist that the Orion records are the work of Elvis, alive and in hiding. *(see also BREWER-GIORGIO, GAYLE and ELVIS IS ALIVE.)*

The Orion material is still on the Sun catalogue.

Overwork

In most discussions of Elvis' death, little is ever said regarding the fact that Elvis was forced, primarily by the Colonel, to work far harder than would ever be normal for an artist of his stature. In 1974, he played 152 shows; in 1975, the total was 106. 1976 saw him doing an even hundred, and up to his death in August 1977, he had performed fifty-four times. When compared with other top rockers of the period like The Who or The Rolling Stones, who might play an eighty-date tour and then lay low for a year or two, Elvis committed himself to a massive workload.

Paget, Debra

Seemingly Elvis was hot to have an affair with Paget, his co-star in the movie *Love Me Tender*, but the fact that Paget was at the time, one of the girlfriends of eccentric billionaire Howard Hughes kept Elvis from making any moves on her. Apparently even Elvis wasn't about to brave the wrath of the unstable and unpredictable Hughes.

Parchman Penitentiary

The Mississippi State Penitentiary at Parchman, the "Parchman farm" of the old blues tune, was where, in 1938–39, Vernon Presley, along with his brother-in-law, Travis Smith, served nine months of a three year sentence for forgery. Vernon and Smith had sold a hog to a local farmer, Orville Bean, for four bucks and then altered the cheque to read $40. Circuit Court Judge Thomas H. Johnson, who had a local reputation for handing down hard time seemed to consider that one month inside for each dollar stolen was reasonable judicial arithmetic. One more lurid version of the tale relates how Vernon received a whipping while at Parchman, the scars of which he carried for the rest of his life. There's also reason to believe that Gladys took Elvis, aged four at the time, to visit his father at the prison. Later in life, Elvis would remark, "My Daddy may seem hard, but you don't know what he's been through."

Parker, Colonel Tom

As one of the principal players in the Elvis Universe, it is impossible in this context to venture in depth into the story of Colonel Tom Parker. Like Priscilla and Gladys, the Colonel is too fundamentally interwoven with the constantly evolving Legend. Ideas of the Colonel's role in the Elvis Universe would appear to take two radically opposing positions. On one hand, the Colonel has been viewed as the roly-poly, lovable hustler who made Elvis a multi-millionaire, for which he should have been profoundly and permanently grateful. Mercifully, this position seems to have become that of a decreasing minority. As the years pass, the Colonel appears more and more like a dark cloud of tastelessness and greed that hung over Elvis' career, exploiting the lowest common factor in

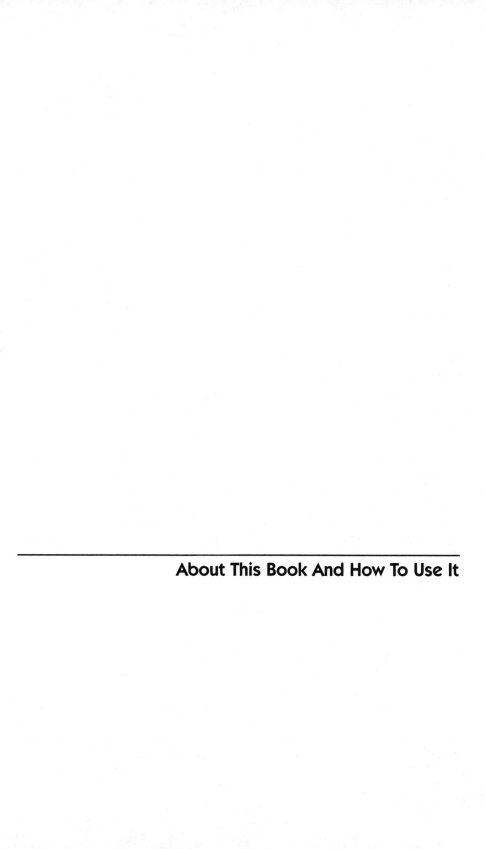

About This Book And How To Use It

every situation, playing upon the worst flaws and weaknesses in Elvis' personality, and at every turn, acting like a spoiler and commercial vandal who seemed driven to short change both the audience and even the popular culture in which Elvis was such a crucial figure.

As the Elvis Presley story becomes more legend than reality, the temptation is to cast Colonel Parker as the Devil. This would be a mistake. The Colonel was ultimately too small time, cheap, and incompetent to play the role of Lucifer. Also, unlike Lucifer, he would end his days in lonely obscurity, after a Tennessee court stripped him of all involvement in the Elvis Presley estate. A more accurate assessment of Parker has to be that, if Elvis was in fact his own worst enemy, the Colonel was a constant malevolent voice, urging him to always make the most self destructive move. *(see also ELVIS AND THE COLONEL and TUAL, BLANCHARD L.)*

Patterson, Aaron Elvis Presley

Born in 1978, the year after Elvis' death, Baby Aaron Patterson was promoted by his mother Deborah Patterson as the reincarnation of Elvis. The public was urged to mail in 20 bucks for which they would receive a membership card to the Baby Elvis Fan Club, a Baby Elvis newsletter, and a Baby Elvis "Living Tribute to The King" T-shirt.

Although plainly bogus, these "Baby Elvis" artifacts are probably quite valuable to some Elvis memorabilia collectors.

Pepsi Cola

Elvis' favourite brand of soda, and according to some accounts, the inspiration for the song "All Shook Up."

Perkins, Carl

Much has been made of how Carl Perkins, the composer of "Blue Suede Shoes," might have been a serious rival to Elvis had he not been seriously injured en route to "The Ed Sullivan Show" in the March 7, 1956 car crash that took the life of his brother. Although undisputedly one of the truly great pioneers of rock & roll, Perkins never had either the looks or the style to seriously rival Elvis or to breakthrough to superstardom in his own right. Perkins himself seemed to be well aware of this fact. "The boy had everything. He had the looks, the moves, the manager, and the talent. And he didn't look like Mr. Ed, like a lot of us did."

Peters, Vicki

Vicki Peters dated Elvis in 1971, and in the same year, blew the whistle on how Elvis had a drug habit. The story appeared in the October 24, 1971 issue of the *Nation Insider*, and was the first public exposure that Elvis was having anything to do with drugs.

Phil Silvers Show, The

A 1957 episode of "The Phil Silvers Show" titled "Rock & Roll Rookie" featured a character called Elvin Pelvin, a rock star parody of Elvis whose big hit was "You Ain't Nothing But A Raccoon." After being drafted, Pelvin is assigned to Sergeant Bilko's platoon. Needless to say, the rest of the plot is devoted to Bilko's efforts to exploit Pelvin, become his manager and get his hands on the rocker's money by any means necessary.

Phonographs

In 1956, confronted by Elvis' phenomenal record sales, RCA decided to complete the circle and market Elvis Presley record players. Two models went on sale that year. For $32.95, fans could buy the Elvis Presley Autographed Special four-speed portable Victrola, the 7EP45, with Elvis' name stamped in gold on the lid. As an added incentive, it came with a double EP of eight tracks from his first album, including "Blue Suede Shoes." For those with $47.95 to throw around, the deluxe model, 7EP2, had an autochanger and not only came with the double EP but also a sampler album *Elvis Presley – Perfect for Parties* on which Elvis crooned "Love Me" and then went on to introduce tracks by Tony Scott, Tito Puente, The Three Suns, and Dave Pell, all RCA hopefuls of the time.

The Elvis Victrolas are now collectors' items.

Plates

The Bradford Exchange, a mail order operation that markets commemorative plates and other limited edition ceramic items, has produced a series of plates, eight-and-a-half inches in diameter, featuring full colour paintings by artists Bruce Emmett, Nate Giorgio, and David Zwierz of Elvis at various stages in his career.

The first plate, *Elvis At The Gates Of Graceland*, was issued in 1988 and is no longer available. The second, *Jailhouse Rock*, is also out of production. The others include: *Elvis*, which shows Elvis in his leather suit on the NBC TV special; *King of Las Vegas*, with Elvis in his white Vegas costume; *Hound Dog* shows Elvis on-stage in his gold jacket; *Love Me Tender* is a romantic portrait of the young Elvis; *Heartbreak Hotel*, described elsewhere in this book; *Blue Suede Shoes*, with Elvis on the "Milton Berle Show"; and *King Creole*, which shows Elvis looking sultry on the set of the movie, were still on sale at the time

of this book's writing, although the Bradford Exchange advertising makes a big deal out of how these items are all from "limited firings."

Two Bradford Exchange Elvis plates appear on the walls of the fictional Conners' home in the TV sitcom, "Roseanne." *(see also HEARTBREAK HOTEL and WOMAN WHO LOVED ELVIS, THE.)*

Contact the Bradford Exchange toll free at 1-800-541-8811.

Playing cards

Over the years, a half-dozen or so packs of Elvis playing cards have appeared on the market. Some have featured fifty-two different pictures of Elvis on the face side of the cards, while other, cheaper packs, simply have a single picture of Elvis on the back.

Available in souvenir and novelty stores.

Pocket knife

An Elvis pocket knife appeared on the market in the mid-eighties and continues to be sold today. It bears a sixties-style picture of Elvis and reads "Elvis Presley, King Of Rock 'n' Roll, 1935-1977." The blade is unusually sharp.
Available at collector and novelty stores.

Pork chops and gravy

Elvis' favourite meat dish.

Pravda

Elvis has appeared on the cover of hundreds of thousands of magazines. Undoubtedly, one of the strangest was when he graced the cover of the December 1987 edition of the monthly English language edition of *Pravda*, the former official Soviet newspaper.

The Soviets always had a hard time with Elvis. The Kremlin never seemed to be able quite to make up its collective mind as to whether both Elvis and rock & roll were the voice of oppressed proletarian youth or a symptom of capitalist decadence. The cover story in *Pravda* titled, "Elvis the King and the Victim" seemed to lean strongly towards the latter. The final paragraphs demonstrate *Pravda*'s bleak view of the King/Victim:

"During the twenty-five years that his career spanned, he did not develop much from the artistic point of view. He had neither the desire nor the courage to venture beyond what the producers offered him on a plate. In all fairness, we must say that he was a product of a certain society and he gave that society what it wanted. The mere fact that so many Americans idolised him is a sad comment on how they see themselves."

Copies of the Elvis edition of *Pravda* are understandably hard to obtain, although a great gift for the Elvis collector who has everything.

Prescription House

Memphis landmark.

The Prescription House at 1737 Madison was where Elvis had his prescriptions filled, including those for the drugs that killed him.

Presley, Andrew

Andrew Presley, Elvis' great-great-great-great-great-grandfather immigrated from Scotland in 1745 and settled in Anson County, North Carolina. His son, Andrew Jr., was a soldier in the Continental Army and fought in the Revolutionary War.

MONTHLY ENGLISH LANGUAGE EDITION

December 1987 (No. 12)
USA $1.95 Canada $2.50 UK 95p.

PRAVDA

ELVIS
the legend
lives on.

Moscow besieged
by motorbike mania.
Family violence
erupts in Canada.

Presley Burger, The

Through the early eighties, a rumour circulated in the punk rock sub-world that Elvis' body had been secretly removed from its coffin prior to burial and a dummy of the correct weight was substituted. Elvis' body was then ground into hamburger and sold on a per ounce basis to a select group of very famous and very decadent rock & roll megastars who subsequently ate it as part of a series of quasi-religious rituals.

Presley, Jr., Dunnan

The great-great-grandfather of Elvis, born in Madisonville, Tennessee, in 1827, seems to have been something of a black sheep, having married four times and deserted the Army of the Confederacy twice.

Presley, Elvis

The Fountainhead. The departed centre of the Elvis Universe. To say more would be redundant.

Elvis and Gladys Presley

Presley, Gladys

Second only to Elvis himself in importance in the Elvis legend, his devoted and protective mother has taken on an almost saintly role in the mythology that is unlikely to ever be revised or diminished. As with Colonel Parker and Priscilla, there is no way, in the context of this book that to delve into the fullness of the relationship between Elvis and his mother. The details have, however been excellently chronicled in the book *Elvis And Gladys* by Elaine Dundy. *(see ELVIS AND GLADYS.)*

Presley, Jesse Garon

In reality, there is little to tell about Jesse Garon Presley. He was delivered stillborn some thirty-five minutes before Elvis' birth. The tiny body was laid in a cardboard box and placed in the living room of the Presley's Tupelo home. The next day, the dead baby, still in the makeshift cardboard coffin, was buried in an unmarked grave in Priceville Cemetery outside Tupelo. The grave was supposed to have been close to a tree. The grave of Elvis twin remains unmarked to this day. Apparently, it was decided after Elvis rose to fame, to leave it that way to discourage sensation-seekers. A commemorative plaque to Jesse Garon was placed in the Meditation Gardens at Graceland, although the name on the plaque is misspelled Jessie Garon Presley.

The role of Jesse Garon in the saga of Elvis Presley is one of total mythology. The idea that twins were somehow special beings is as old as humanity, and it has always been believed that, when one twin dies, it has profound effect on the other. These ancient beliefs have been effectively woven into the Elvis legend by writers, artists and filmmakers. In the TV movie *Elvis*, Elvis played by Kurt Russell, holds conversations with his dead brother. The idea of the incomplete surviving twin is also explored in Nick Cave's musical piece "The Firstborn Is Dead." At its most extreme, psychic Bill Falcone claims to have "channeled" Elvis describing the internal conflict as the Elvis spirit and the Jesse Garon spirit battled for control of the single living body. All these fixations with the deceased twin appear to be a form of support to the idea that Elvis' power can only be explained by his being some kind of supernatural being *(see also CAVE, NICK; FALCONE, BILL; and PRICEVILLE CEMETERY.)*

Presley, Lisa Marie

Aside from the fact that she actually existed and was photographed as a newborn being stared at fondly by her proud parents, Elvis' daughter Lisa Marie only figured in the Elvis legend in the most minor way. After Elvis' death, her picture would now and again appear in the gossip columns—a sullen, slack-faced, rather pouty teenager with the same "dishwater blonde" hair as her father, usually hurrying through an airport or a hotel lobby accompanied by her mom. Rumours circulated that she was something of a troubled teen, being moved from one private school to another, one jump ahead of an alleged obsession with boys and drugs. For the most part, however, Lisa Marie was kept well under wraps while her father became the stuff of mythology, and her mother co-starred in "Dallas," and took on the reorganisation of the Presley estate.

CHELSEA CLINTON • ERIC CLAPTON • ROBERT BLAKE

MARCH 1, 1993 $2.29

People
weekly

Elvis with 3-year-old
Lisa Marie in 1971

ELVIS' BABY GIRL

This month,
LISA MARIE PRESLEY
turned 25 and
inherited her dad's
$100 million estate.
What's next?
More kids and (yes!)
a singing career

Like her mother, she was reputed to be heavy into Scientology.

The picture changed somewhat on 8 January 1993, when Lisa Marie made an unprecedented public appearance at Graceland during the celebrations for the issuing of the Elvis postage stamp. The TV cameras showed a radically altered Lisa Marie. Suddenly, she was her father's daughter with a vengeance. Her hair was now dyed black and piled up on top her head. In black dress and sinister Morticia Addams makeup, Lisa Marie was sultry to the point of vampiric. This public outing was followed up by a cover story in the 1 March 1993 edition of *People* in which the same image was maintained. It almost started to seem that if Elvis worship ever became a full-blown religion, Lisa Marie was well positioned to become the High Priestess of the cult. With her background in Scientology—a religion that began as little more than the fantasy of science fiction writer L. Ron Hubbard—she might be admirably equipped to handle the gig.

At the time of this writing, an extraordinary rumour was starting to spread that Lisa Marie had married Michael Jackson. It started as word of mouth, then moved to television. For some days, it was dismissed as pure fantasy, but then the 26 July issue of the *National Enquirer* broke the story that Lisa Marie and Jackson had indeed gone through a secret ceremony on 26 May 1994, at the home of Judge Hugo Alvarez in the Dominican Republic. Security at the wedding was reputed to be so tight that the Judge's house was professionally searched for hidden recording equipment before the couple would even enter the building. Although tabloid news stories have a lousy reputation for accuracy, U.S. officials in the Dominican Republic seemingly vouch for Alvarez as a well-respected jurist. To back up his claims, Alvarez has even produced copies of the marriage papers.

To date, neither Michael nor Lisa Marie have made any comment confirming or denying the marriage, although in early June of 1994, rumours buzzed around New York that they were staying together at the Trump Towers. Possibly the most confusing aspect of the whole episode is the fact that, although Lisa Marie, as part of the wedding ceremony, signed a declaration that she was "free to marry," as far as anyone has so far been able to ascertain, no records exist to show that she had divorced her estranged husband Danny Keough.

Presley, Priscilla

It has always been a wonder to me that Priscilla Presley managed to stay sane through what must have been a deeply weird life both with and without Elvis. She even went on to become a devotee of Scientology and star in the Leslie Nielsen *Naked Gun* series of comedy films. Priscilla Presley is, however, currently

Illustration from Elvis Presley, *a bio-comic by Tiki and Delmo Waters: Personality Classics*

the ultimate power and authority on at least the temporal and financial plane of the Elvis Universe. No legal product cometh to the market except via her.

Priscilla's own story, including how she spent the early part of her life as Elvis' live-in, underage concubine and subsequently his wife, is fully chronicled, at least from her point of view, in her book *Elvis And Me.*

In Priscilla's favour, it must be said that since Colonel Parker was removed from any controlling role in the Presley Estate and Priscilla took the helm, the Elvis Presley product has gone through a quantum improvement in both quality and dignity. *(see also ELVIS AND ME.)*

Presley's pub

The English have a tradition of naming pubs after famous, usually historical figures. Thus it is no big deal to go for a drink in The Queen Victoria, The Duke Of Wellington, The Earl Percy, or The Charlie Chaplin (a pub in south London). A new twist on this time honoured tradition is Presley's Bar in London's West End.

Presley's Bar is located at 46 Tottenham Court Road, London W1.

Presley, Vernon

It always struck me that Vernon had to be kind of dumb. Almost from the very start, it was clear that Gladys provided the spark and the energy in the Presley household. Even "Elvis," the highly sanitised TV series about Elvis' early years, depicted Vernon as little better than a surly oaf with a bad back who had virtually no faith in his son's potential or talent. It may have been that Vernon had much of the stuffing knocked out of him by the Great Depression, a spell in jail for cheque forgery, and a general lack of education. Certainly Elvis went through great pains to defend his daddy, basically telling critics to try walking a mile in Vernon's shoes. On the other hand, Vernon was able to retire at age thirty-nine and live off his son for the rest of his days.

Gladys, Elvis, and Vernon Presley

Even with Elvis picking up the tab, Vernon doesn't appear to have managed to pull very much together. Elvis paid Vernon $75,000 a year to act as his private business manager, but financial records clearly show that Vernon was hopelessly incompetent. His second marriage to Dee Stanley seemingly didn't sit well with Elvis who became actively pissed off when his new stepmother started to redecorate Graceland.

Vernon Presley died of heart failure on 26 June 1979. He was 63. *(see also I NEVER KNEW A GUITAR PLAYER WHO WAS WORTH A DAMN and PARCHMAN PENITENTIARY.)*

Priceville Cemetery

Elvis' twin, Jesse Garon Presley, is buried in an unmarked grave in Priceville Cemetery, three miles north of Tupelo on Feemster Lake Road. Apparently only a handful of people know the exact location the grave. *(see also PRESLEY, JESSE GARON.)*

Priscilla and Elvis

Paperback book, 1985. By Caroline Latham: Signet.

Yet another unauthorised Elvis bio. This one concentrates on the Presley marriage.

Out of print. Check the used bookstores.

The Prophet

Elvis set great store by this volume of religious philosophy by Khalil Gibran. Since his death, the more extreme Elvis fans have set equally great store by a set of lines from the book that read:

"Brief were my days among you, and briefer were the words I have spoken. But should my voice fade from your ears, and my love vanish in your memory, then I will come again."

QVC

For a period in 1993, the cable-TV home shopping channel ran daily two-hour special segments devoted entirely to Elvis merchandise.

Rainmaker, The

One of the great missed chances.

In 1956, Elvis tested as the juvenile lead to co-star with Katherine Hepburn and Burt Lancaster in the movie *The Rainmaker*. Unfortunately, the Colonel vetoed the idea, feeling that Elvis should take top billing in a film vehicle custom-tailored to his talent and his audience. *The Rainmaker* role went to Earl Holliman; Elvis went to *Love Me Tender* and the world was left to speculate just how different Elvis' acting career might have been if his motion picture debut had been in a serious film, working beside world-class actors. *(see also STAR IS BORN, A; MIDNIGHT COWBOY; and THUNDER ROAD.)*

Rivera, Geraldo

The investigative reporter turned talk show host was largely responsible for blowing the whistle on the dubious circumstances and possible cover-up surrounding Elvis' death. In 1979, Rivera was a reporter on the ABC TV news magazine series "20/20." On the 15 September 1979 edition, Rivera presented a segment titled "The Elvis Cover-Up" that focused on Elvis' drug problems, the massive over-prescribing by Dr. George Nichopoulos, and the attempts that had been made to conceal the true cause of death. Apart from the drug allegations made by Red and Sonny West in their book *Elvis – What Happened?*, it was the first public exposure of the reality of Elvis' final days.

Later, Rivera would make items about Elvis a regular feature on his CBS talk show "Geraldo." *(see also DEATH OF ELVIS, THE; ELVIS – WHAT HAPPENED; and NICHOPOULOS, DR. GEORGE C.)*

Robertson, Jane

When, in 1971, a young woman passed out while she and Elvis were on a Hycadon prescription drug binge and had to be stomach-pumped, she was checked into hospital under the name Jane Robertson.

Rod Building and Customizer

Elvis contributed a short article to the September 1956 edition of the hot rod magazine, *Rod Building And Customizer*. It was titled "Rock N' Roll N' Drag." Copies of the original magazine are now worth a fortune to collectors.

Ryan, Shiela

Elvis dated Sheila Ryan, who appeared on the cover of the October 1973 issue of *Playboy*, through 1975, between his affairs with Linda Thompson and Ginger Alden. A year later, Ms. Ryan would marry movie star James Caan.

Salem, Marc

Four days before Elvis died, Philadelphia psychic Marc Salem wrote a prediction of Elvis' death, including the headlines from both the *Philadelphia Daily News*, "The King Is Dead!" and the *Philadelphia Inquirer*, "The King Dies At 42." He placed the written predictions in an aspirin bottle that was then baked into a pretzel. The entire bizarre process was supervised by former Philadelphia District Attorney Arlen Spector.

By weird coincidence, Spector, who would later be elected to the U.S. Senate had, as an aide to the Warren Commission, been the individual who had invented the Kennedy Assassination "magic bullet" theory—the idea one bullet had passed through the body of President Kennedy and then gone on to injure Texas Governor John Connolly, who was sitting in front of him in the fateful limousine—"proving" that Lee Harvey Oswald was the lone gunman.

Saturday Night Live

Quote—A. Whitney Brown

"He was a poor kid, but he had a rockin' guitar, some flashy clothes and wiggle in his hips—and he had that certain something called 'talent.' Of course he never made a nickel because he was black, but two years later Elvis Presley made a fortune doing the same thing."

Scatter

Elvis owned a pet chimpanzee called Scatter. Unfortunately the chimp became too much of a favourite with the Memphis Mafia. They dressed him in human clothes and started feeding him booze to the point that Scatter developed a taste for straight scotch, became alcoholic and violent, and ultimately died of cirrhosis of the liver.

Scarves

Reproductions of the satin scarves that Elvis used to anoint with his sweat and hand out to front row fans at his concerts can be purchased at the Graceland gift shop. They come in white, pale blue and lavender and bear a facsimile of Elvis' signature in gold.

Shroud of Turin, The

According to most reports, at the time of his death, Elvis was seated on the toilet reading *The Shroud Of Turin* by Ian Wilson. Counter-claims do, however, maintain that the book he took into the bathroom with him was actually *The Scientific Search For The Face Of Jesus* by Frank Adams.

Sideburns

As every Elvis imitator knows, sideburns were one of the great Elvis Presley visual trademarks. It was a style that he claimed to have copied from the long distance truck drivers of the early fifties that he saw as a teenager in and around Memphis.

What every Elvis imitator doesn't know is that sideburns were named for Ambrose Everett Burnside, the Union General who wore lavish sidewhiskers and had to resign in 1862 after he screwed up royally at the Battle of Fredricksburg.

Sightings

At the peak of the "Elvis is alive" furor of the late eighties, individuals began reporting Elvis sightings much in the manner of Bigfoot, UFOs or the Loch Ness Monster. Elvis was spotted in places as far apart as Hawaii and Baltimore, and oddly, these sightings invariably took place in locations like lunch counters, the checkout lines at supermarkets and hamburger joints, places that, in life, Elvis would never have been able to go. Obviously many of these so-called sightings were nothing more than products of the imagination of tabloid writers. The law of averages does dictate, though, that a percentage of these had to be real, at least in the mind of the sightee.

Through the late eighties and early nineties, the idea of Elvis sightings and Elvis as some kind of supernatural entity thoroughly permeated the pop culture. A perfect example of this was Fox TV sitcom "Married With Children" that devoted an entire 1992 episode to Peg Bundy experiencing an Elvis sighting. *(see also IS ELVIS ALIVE.)*

Sinatra, Frank

TONIGHT 9:30-10:30 CH 5-33-49

ELVIS PRESLEY RETURNS TO TV

AS SPECIAL GUEST STAR ON THE

FRANK SINATRA-TIMEX SHOW

PLUS

SAMMY DAVIS, JR.·JOEY BISHOP·NANCY SINATRA AND OTHERS

More People Buy

TIMEX Than Any Other Watch In the World

In 1957, Frank Sinatra made the following statement to the press, "Rock & roll smells phony and false. It is sung, played, and written for the most part by cretinous goons, and by means of its almost imbecilic reiteration, and sly, lewd, in plain fact, dirty lyrics, it manages to be the martial music of every sideburned delinquent on the face of the earth. It is the most brutal, ugly, desperate, vicious form of expression it has been my misfortune to hear."

For awhile, it seemed as though a feud was going to break out between crooner and rocker, but then, at a press conference, Elvis somewhat defused the situation by not rising to the bait. "I admire the man. He has a right to his opinion." By 1960, however, Sinatra had totally changed his tune. Now Sinatra was devoting his entire 15 May TV show to welcoming Elvis home from the Army, and even singing duets with him. Maybe, to Frank, Elvis had redeemed himself by his stint in the Army, or maybe the ratings talked louder than musical prejudices.

Sinatra, Nancy

Nancy Sinatra co-starred in one Elvis movie—*Speedway.* From 1960 onwards, when she appeared on her father's "Welcome home Elvis" TV show, rumours abounded that she and Elvis were having an affair.

Sixteen coaches

"Train I ride, sixteen coaches long."
In a bizarre echo of the line in the song "Mystery Train," Elvis' funeral procession consisted of sixteen white limousines.

Slaughter, Todd

Prominent British fan who took over the publication of *Elvis Monthly* after the death of its founder, Albert Hand.

Sleepwalking

According to contemporary stories, Elvis and both his parents suffered serious problems with sleepwalking, particularly in the period 1939–40 immediately after Vernon was released from jail. When awakened, they would also have no memory of what had happened. Elvis' sleepwalking would seem to have definitely persisted, at least until the time that he was drafted. It may well have continued through his entire life. If that is true, a case might be made that, in part, Elvis' drug problems may even have been a result of continuing sleep disorders. *(see also INSOMNIA.)*

Social Security number

Elvis' Social Security number was 409-52-2002. Fans obsessed by numerology note that the last four digits are 2001 + one. *(see also TWO THOUSAND AND ONE.)*

Socks

You want socks with Elvis' signature on them? Or a picture of Elvis? They exist.
   Available at novelty and clothing stores.

Sounding Story, The

Book, 1959. By Peter de Vecchi.
   The first book ever written about Elvis was in German.
   Copies are so rare that they are virtually unobtainable.

Spector, Phil

Phil Spector, genius record producer, rock & roll eccentric, and creator of the "Phil Spector Wall Of Sound" was able to produce the Beatles, but never got to produce Elvis, something that was a lifelong disappointment to him. Spector also believed that Colonel Tom Parker had Elvis under hypnotic mind control. Although it sounds a little fantastic and paranoid, Parker was seemingly able to hypnotise people, a knack that he picked up during his carnival days and frequently used to humiliate his underlings.

Spoons

Fan souvenir, 1994.
   What exactly the connection between Elvis Presley and a set of spoons is escapes me, except that it may be the definitive proof that there are people out there who will market just about anything with a picture of Elvis on it. At least three "silvertone" Elvis spoons are currently on the market.
   Available from Graceland Gifts, 3734 Elvis Presley Boulevard, Memphis, TN 38116.

Stammer

Elvis was prone to stammering under stress, and indeed, he can be heard doing it for a moment on the soundtrack of the movie *Kissin' Cousins*. The stammer, however, only affected his speaking voice. When singing, he had perfect control.

Stamp

The issue of the Elvis Presley 29 cent postage stamp on 5 January 1993 seemed to mark some kind of watershed in the posthumous career of Elvis Presley. Prior to the issue of the stamp, a definite fading had been noticeable. The media, particularly TV, still cobbled together some kind of tribute on his birthday on 8 January, and on the 16 August anniversary of his death. But for the most part, the general perception was that, after Elvis had been dead for a full decade-and-a-half, the public was about ready to move on to more contemporary considerations. In fact, this general media perception couldn't have been more wrong. 8 January 1993 was a cold, wet day in most parts of the U.S., and yet in almost unbelievable TV coverage, the nation watched as tens of thousands of otherwise rational people waited all night in the rain and snow to be first on their block to have an Elvis stamp franked with a first day postmark. Elvis imitators performed in normally sedate and serious post offices, and the U.S. Postal Service and the Elvis Presley Estate joined forces with Turner Broadcasting to throw a televised celebration that featured, as the culmination of thirty-six hours of non-stop programming, the first ever major public appearance by Lisa Marie Presley in her capacity as Elvis' daughter and heir. It suddenly seemed as though a new wave of Elvis devotion was sweeping the country. The most amazing part was that it had been triggered not by Elvis' music or movies, but by something as seemingly trivial as a 29 cent stamp. More had to be at work here than merely philately or nostalgia for a dead entertainer.

Not that Elvis exactly appeared out of the blue, the hoopla leading up to the issue of the stamp had been going on for sometime. The Postal Service had first organized a design competition that eventually narrowed the field down to two designs, one of a young rockabilly and one of an older Vegas incarnation. These designs by artist Mark Stutzman were unveiled at a gala publicity bash at the Las Vegas Hilton hosted by Wayne Newton and the Colonel (making one last stand, as though to demonstrate that no matter what the courts might say, he was still in the Elvis business). It was then announced that the final decision as to which image of Elvis would appear on the stamp would be left to the general public. The Postal Service was going to organize an Elvis stamp election.

Far from being viewed as possibly verging on madness, the choice of the Elvis stamp was accepted as a legitimate question facing the nation. When yellow ballot cards, showing the two designs, appeared in Post Offices on 6 April 1992, they vanished almost immediately. When Bill Clinton, running for office at the time, appeared on "The Arsenio Hall Show," he was quizzed as to his preference. Clinton opted for the young Elvis and in so doing predicted the ultimate choice of the country.

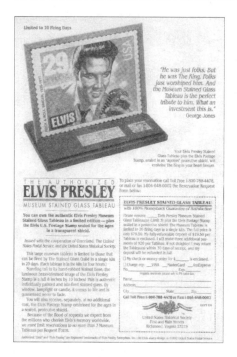

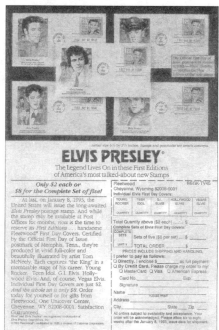

Ironically, the Elvis stamp almost never saw the light of day. Almost immediately after Elvis' death, fans started lobbying for him to be commemorated on a postage stamp. Nothing could be done however, until 1987 at the earliest, because one of the primary rules of the Postal Service was that, to get on a stamp, you have to have been dead for ten years or more. The Elvis stamp project was the brainchild of the then Postmaster General Anthony Frank, but all new stamp designs have to he approved at the Citizens Stamp Advisor Committee, some of whom felt that Elvis, after the revelations of his drug use and the circumstances of his death, was hardly a suitable subject. Only a major effort of will on Frank's part pushed the concept through the committee.

Possibly the weirdest part of the whole Elvis stamp phenomenon was the marketing boom that the stamp triggered. First off the line, with stamp related merchandise was the Postal Service itself. It issued a catalogue and 800 number (1-800-STAMP-24) offering the following items:

Elvis Stamp Sheet And Saver Sleeve: "A sheet of forty mint-condition Elvis stamps in a sleeve reminiscent of a record album dust jacket."

Elvis Commemorative Album: "This specially commissioned story of the King's life charts his rise to stardom through sixteen pages of little-known facts and rare photos. Includes hardcover slip jacket and block of four mint stamps."

Elvis Limited-Edition Print: "A full colour, 12"x12" reproduction of stamp designer Mark Stutzman's Young Elvis' portrait. Includes an Elvis U.S. stamp and 'first day of issue' Graceland cancellation."

Exclusive "First Day" Ceremony Programme: From the Graceland 'first day of issue' ceremony, a limited run of this special programme. Includes the Elvis stamp with Graceland cancellation, plus the day's agenda."

The Postal Service may have been the first out of the box with their line of souvenirs, but many others were right behind them. For awhile, it seemed that one could hardly turn around without bumping into a reproduction of the Elvis stamp on anything from towels to watches. Graceland Gifts put out an entire catalogue of stamp related items and, at the other end of the scale, street vendors were handing out poorly printed, unofficial stamp T-shirts. What follows is a list of objects offered for sale bearing a likeness of the Elvis stamp. It is as complete as possible, but there may be more lurking out there:

Gold stamp replica
Music box
Watch
Earrings
Tie tack
Clock
Poster
Key ring
Spoon
Letter Opener
Beer Stein
Christmas tree ornament
License plate
Jigsaw puzzle
Stained glass panel
Pillow
T-shirt
Sweatshirt
Nightshirt
Baseball cap
Oven mitt
Potholder
Bath Set
Beach Towel
Fridge magnet
Glassware
Drinking mug

Of course, the most obvious souvenir and, at 29 cents, the cheapest, is the stamp itself.

Stanek, Leslie

On 16 November 1990, devoted British fan Leslie Stanek, legally changed his name to Elvis Aron Presley.

Stanley, Dee

Dee Stanley was the second wife of Vernon Presley. Most accounts indicate that Elvis disliked her. Whether that was a matter of her personality, or whether it was simply because he subconsciously felt that she had displaced his mother is a matter of conjecture. Like most of the Presley inner circle, she wrote a book, *Elvis We Love You Tender*, after his death. She divorced Vernon in 1977 and married a younger man.

Star is Born, A

One of the great missed chances.

Barbra Streisand wanted Elvis to co-star with her in the 1976, fourth movie version of *A Star Is Born*. Yet again, the Colonel held out for too much money. His basic greed killed the project as far as Elvis was concerned, and Kris Kristofferson got the part. We can only speculate what such a major dramatic role would have done for Elvis at that low ebb-point in his career. It might even have saved his life. *(see also MIDNIGHT COWBOY; RAINMAKER, THE; and THUNDER ROAD.)*

Star Wars

Elvis spent some of his last day on Earth trying to get hold of a print of *Star Wars* to run for Lisa Marie. None were available and clearly the Force was not with him. Elvis also had some dental work done the same day.

Stationery

A considerable quantity of Elvis stationery is currently on the market—pens, pencils, notepaper, binders, rubber stamps, note books, address books, diaries, checkbook covers, and a number of Elvis paperweights. It seems that it might be possible to equip an entire office with Elvis stuff.

Available at souvenir, stationery and department stores.

Statue of Liberty

The 1986 celebrations marking both the centennial and restoration of the Statue of Liberty culminated in a spectacular live variety show and firework display at Liberty Island in New York Harbour that featured a coordinated display by two hundred massed Elvis impersonators. The event was the brainchild of producer Alan Carr.

Stone, Mike

The great irony when Priscilla ran off with her karate instructor Mike Stone, was that Elvis had introduced them in the first place. Stone, who had previously been Phil Spector's bodyguard, was working at the time on the security team at the Las Vegas International Hilton, and it was at Elvis' suggestion that Priscilla began taking karate lessons from him. The two initially became friends, then lovers, and ultimately moved in together at an apartment in Huntington Beach in Los Angeles.

According to Sonny West, Elvis was so enraged at Priscilla's desertion that he attempted to put out a hit on Stone, and it was only with great difficulty that the Memphis Mafia was able to persuade him that the commission of a homicide represented a line that not even Elvis could afford to cross.

A weird side effect of the situation was that from the time Priscilla left him, Elvis refused to watch the TV show "Streets Of San Francisco" because the Karl Malden character was named Mike Stone.

Storm, Tempest

Tempest Storm was one of the legendary strippers of the 1950s, and according to her autobiography *The Lady Is A Vamp*, published in 1987, she claimed to have enjoyed a wild week-long affair with Elvis in Las Vegas in 1957, during which Elvis, at one point, climbed a fence and broke into her hotel room at 3 A.M. to be with her.

Suicide

Perhaps in order to cash in on Elvis one last time, Albert Goldman, author of the notorious hatchet-job biography *Elvis*, came out with a 1990 cover story in *Life* claiming that Elvis committed suicide. Aside from Elvis' massive intake of pills, Goldman seemed to base his entire theory around a

Tempest Storm

remark allegedly made by Elvis to employee/stepbrother David Stanley a few weeks before his death. "I'd rather be unconscious than miserable." By this point, however, Goldman's credibility was so low both with musicologists and Elvis fans that few took his idea seriously.

Sullivan, Ed

Elvis appeared three times on "The Ed Sullivan Show"—the TV show that was famous for maintaining the standards of American decency by only shooting Elvis from the waist up. He received record ratings even though Ed Sullivan had originally stated that he would never allow Elvis on his show.

In fact, Sullivan himself did not appear on the Elvis debut show. He had been injured in an automobile accident, and Charles Laughton was brought in as the substitute host.

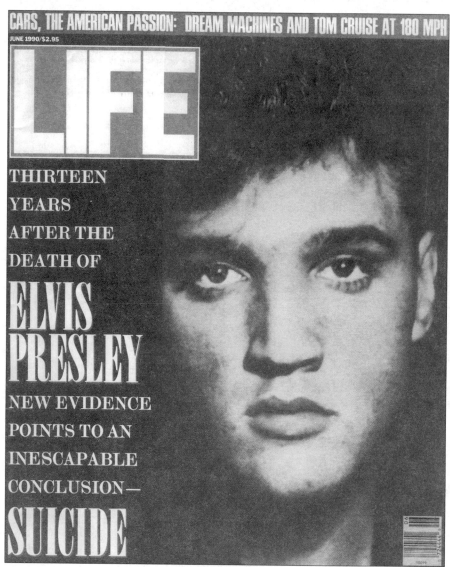

CARS, THE AMERICAN PASSION: DREAM MACHINES AND TOM CRUISE AT 180 MPH

JUNE 1990/$2.95

LIFE

THIRTEEN
YEARS
AFTER THE
DEATH OF

ELVIS
PRESLEY

NEW EVIDENCE
POINTS TO AN
INESCAPABLE
CONCLUSION—

SUICIDE

Life's "suicide" issue

Sunglasses

You want to wear a pair of those thick, metal rimmed aviator sunglasses just like every Elvis imitator on the planet? Graceland Gifts has them. In silver-tone or gold-tone finish.

Graceland Gifts, 1-800-238-2000

Sun Records (landmark)

Memphis landmark.

The historic building at 706 Union Street was almost lost to music historians and Elvis fans when in 1969, Shelby Singleton bought the company from Sam Phillips and transferred operations to Nashvllle. For awhile, the premises were used by a plumbing company and an auto-parts store. Then, in the late seventies, it was restored to a facsimile of the original recording studio by Grayline Tours and is now a tourist attraction and a protected landmark.

Sun Records (recordings)

The lost recordings.

According to legend, the following songs were recorded by Elvis while under contract to Sam Phillips but never released—"Always Late," "Blue Guitar," "Crying Heart Blues," "I Got A Woman," "Maybelline," "Down The Line," "Satisfied," "Give Me More, More, More," "Gone," "Night Train To Memphis," "Tennessee Saturday Night," "That's The Stuff You Gotta Watch," and "Uncle Penn."

Fans have always hoped that someday these masters would be unearthed and released much in the manner of *The Million Dollar Quartet*, but after all this time, the likelihood of that happening is just about zero. It's possible that Sam Phillips may actually have recorded over the tapes, something he did in the early days to reduce overheads. *(see also MILLION DOLLAR QUARTET, THE.)*

Sweat

This is essentially a postcard-sized bubble pack containing a small plastic vial of what jokingly purports to be Elvis' sweat. This tasteless little item first appeared in 1985, and despite pressure from the Estate that it should be discontinued, it is still on sale today.

Manufactured by Maiden Jestz Inc. Available in card shops and joke and novelty stores.

Swing set

On the "The Late Show with David Letterman," actress Susan Sarandon recounted the story of how when she received a private tour of Graceland while filming the 1994 movie *The Client* in Memphis, she noticed that Lisa Marie's old outdoor swing set was riddled with bullet holes. It seems that Elvis made a habit of taking potshots at the swing set from the small balcony outside his bedroom. Needless to say, Lisa Marie was not using the swing set at the time. *(see also GUNS.)*

Tapestry

Manufactured in the Far East and sold in discount stores and flea markets, cheap tapestries—garish but with a definite pop art charm—have existed since the early eighties. They come in three manor designs, two Vegas images and one head shot based on a promo photo from *King Creole*. Over the years, the Elvis tapestries have also been incorporated into clothing such as the back panels of coats and jackets.

Taylor's Restaurant

Memphis landmark.

Taylor's Restaurant, an American diner of the most satisfyingly traditional kind, stands right next door to the Sun Records recording studio at 710 Union Street. It was the hangout and unofficial commissary for Sun Recording artists, including Elvis, during Sun's heyday in the mid-fifties. Now it feeds tourists taking the Grayline "Elvis" tour.

TCB

The letters TCB—standing for "Taking Care of Business"— arranged around a lightning bolt became the logo of all Elvis Presley operations during the 1970s. The logo was designed by Lee Ableseron, the partner of jewelry dealer Sol Schwartz. The Memphis Mafia were all given ID bracelets that carried the emblem and their respective nicknames. Later, they would receive pendants and other jewelry of the same design. Elvis was buried wearing a diamond TCB ring.

According to backup singer Kathy Westmoreland, Elvis adopted the lightning bolt insignia after lightning struck a marble statue in the Meditation Gardens at Graceland. Priscilla claims that she and Elvis decided on the lightning bolt logo while riding through a thunderstorm in a plane. The lightning bolt is, however, almost identical to the one in the comic books that turned crippled newsboy Freddy Freeman into Captain Marvel, Jr., which, knowing the young Elvis' obsession with Captain Marvel, Jr., seems a far more likely explanation. *(see also CAPTAIN MARVEL, JR. and MEDITATION GARDENS.)*

Various reproductions of TCB Jewelry is available mail order from Graceland Gifts 1-800-238-2000.

TCB Band

This was name given to the band that backed Elvis through the 1970s. The solid core of the band was James Burton (guitar), Jerry Scheff (guitar), John Wilkinson (rhythm guitar), Joe Osbourne (bass), Hal Blaine (drums), Ronnie Tutt (drums), Glen D. Hardin (piano), Marty Harrel (trombone), and Pat Houston (trumpet). In the early eighties, the same band would be hired to back Elvis Costello at a special concert.

Teddy Bears

In 1956, Elvis received 282 stuffed bears as Christmas gifts from fans.

Tennessee tourist commercial

TV commercial, spring 1994.

In March of 1994, the Tennessee Tourist Board launched a campaign to promote tourism in the state spearheaded by an animated TV commercial in which the figure on the Elvis postage stamp came alive and began singing and gyrating. A spokesperson for the campaign pointed out that "no one says Tennessee like Elvis." In fact the voice of Elvis was recreated by leading Elvis sound-a-like Ronnie McDowell.

Texaco

With a 1993 gasoline TV commercial that showed a sideburned figure lurking in a Texaco station, the oil company joined the list of numerous corporations and advertisers who have used the belief that Elvis is alive as a promotional gimmick. *(see also SIGHTINGS.)*

This Is Elvis

Documentary film produced by David L. Wolper.

Using a great deal of previously unseen live and backstage concert footage of Elvis and dramatic recreations of his early life, *This Is Elvis* is a largely accurate and wholly dignified record of the life and work of Elvis Presley that totally stands up as cinematic record of the man and his music.

Available on videocassette with an added 43 minutes that were not included in the theatrical release.

Thompson, Linda

Model and actress Linda Thompson, who held the titles "Miss Liberty Bowl" and "Miss Memphis State," lived at Graceland with Elvis for four-and-a-half years between 1972 and 1976. During this time, it's been estimated that Elvis spent over a million dollars on jewelry and gifts for Ms. Thompson, and just prior to their breaking up, she is supposed to have run up bills of over $30,000 on his credit cards.

Her story is that she left Elvis because she couldn't sit around and watch him self destruct on drugs, although, in another account, it was seemingly his weird nocturnal habits that started to get to her. "I couldn't stand living like a bat." Less charitable third party accounts suggest that Linda Thompson didn't leave Elvis at all, but that he had members of the Memphis Mafia "throw her out" of Graceland.

Thunder Road

One of the great missed chances.

In 1958, Robert Mitchum offered Elvis a co-starring role as his brother in *Thunder Road*, the classic action film about bootleggers. The Colonel declined. Elvis wasn't co-starring with anyone, even if he might be moving closer to his goal as being considered as a serious actor. The part was played by Mitchum's son James. *(see also STAR IS BORN, A; MIDNIGHT COWBOY; and RAIN-MAKER, THE.)*

Ties

Yes, my friends, we even have Elvis ties. Indeed, there have been Elvis ties for as long as there's been Elvis. Widely published publicity pictures of Marianne Faithfull taken around 1967 showing Marianne wearing a man's shirt and a wide satin Elvis tie.

Contemporary Elvis ties—including a pair of rather nice collage ties are available in souvenir stores.

Tour jacket

Originally manufactured for the crew on the concert tour that never was, the one that was about to start at the time of Elvis' death, these jackets are now offered for sale—and at $299.95, are one of the most expensive pieces of Elvis merchandise on the market. The varsity-style jacket has a red wool body and cream leather sleeves and carries the legend "ELVIS—IN

CONCERT" and the TCB (Taking Care of Business) lightning flash logo. *(see also TCB.)*

Mail order from Hammacher Schlemmer, P.O. Box 182256, Chattanooga, TN 37422-7256.

Toothpick holder

The Graceland Gifts catalogue for Spring/Summer 1994 features an Elvis toothpick holder, a white cylindrical mini-mug with the legend "Elvis Presley 1935–1977." This may well qualify as the most banal and idiotic Elvis souvenir of all time—too chincy to even be tasteless. Back when I was kid, the greasers who loved Elvis—the guys who wanted to be him and the girls who wanted to fuck him—would never have even considered owning any kind of toothpick holder of any kind, let alone an Elvis toothpick holder. Toothpicks came from dispensers beside the cash register in the diner, and Elvis was a rebel in the cause of rock & roll. A toothpick holder? Gimme a break!

Graceland gifts, 1-800-238-2000.

Towels

Elvis' image even appears on towels of all colours and qualities.

Available in souvenir, novelty and department stores.

True Romance

Feature film, 1993. Christian Slater, Patricia Arquette. Dennis Hopper, Gary Oldman, Brad Pitt, Bronson Pinchot. Directed by Tony Scott.

The spectral figure of Elvis appears at crucial moments in this action, chase, cocaine, and murder movie to advise the hero Clarence (Christian Slater) what he ought to do next, much in the manner of the Humphrey Bogart figure in Woody Allen's *Play It Again Sam.*

Available on videocassette.

Truth About Me, The

Limited edition single (RCA SP-8705)

On Sunday, 9 September 1956, Elvis was booked to make his first appearance on Ed Sullivan's "Talk Of The Town"—at the time, the ultimate prestige TV variety show (also the show where Sullivan issued his legendary directive that Elvis was to only be photographed from the waist up.)

To mark the event, *TV Guide* put Elvis on the cover of the September 8–14 issue and collaborated with RCA to issue 500 copies of a limited edition "interview" single that would be mailed out to major radio stations along with a sheet of questions that could be inserted prior to Elvis' pre-recorded answers. Security was tight on these pressings. Instructions were that the composite "interviews" should only be broadcast 8–14 September and after that, the discs should be returned to RCA. On no account should the discs be made available to the general public.

A few months later, a slightly different situation occurred in the United Kingdom where the magazine *Reveille*, a weekly tabloid of the time, offered the same recording, on a poorly pressed, five inch disc, as a mail order special offer titled—"Elvis Presley – The Truth About Me."

Copies of these records are now virtually unobtainable, although the actual recording has been widely bootlegged and a slightly different edit of it appeared in 1979 on *Elvis—A Legendary Performer Vol. 3* (U.S. RCA CPL 1-3082).

The complete text of "The Truth About Me" as it appeared on the original disc, is as follows:

> Hi, this is Elvis Presley. I guess the first thing people want to know is why I can't stand still when I'm singing. Some people tap their feet, some people snap their fingers, and some just sway back and forth. I just started doing them all together, I guess. Singing rhythm and blues really knocks it out. I watch my audiences and I listen to them and I know we're all getting something out of our system but none of us knows what it is. The important thing is that we're getting rid of it and nobody's getting hurt.

I suppose you know I've got a lot of cars. People have written about it in the papers and a lot of them ask me why. Well, when I was driving a truck, every time a big shiny car drove by, it started me sort of daydreaming. I always felt that some day, somehow, something would happen to change everything for me, and I'd daydream about how it would be.

The first car I ever bought was the most beautiful car I'd ever seen. It was second hand, but I parked it outside my hotel the day I got it and stayed up all night just looking at it. And the next day it caught fire and burned upon the road.

In a lot of the mail I get, people ask questions about the kind of things I do and that sort of stuff. Well, I don't smoke and I don't drink and I like to go to movies. Maybe some day, I'm gonna have a home and a family of my own and I won't budge from it. I was an only child, but maybe my kids won't be. I suppose this kind of talk raises another question: Am I in love? No. I've thought I've been in love, but I guess I wasn't. It just passed over. I guess I haven't met the girl yet, but I will and I hope it won't be too long because I get lonesome sometimes. I get lonesome right in the middle of a crowd. I get a feeling that, with her, whoever she may be, I won't be lonesome any more.

Well, thanks for letting me talk and sort of get things off my chest. I want to thank all my loyal fans who watch my performances and who, in a way, have become friends of mine. I sure appreciate you listening to my RCA Victor records and I would like to thank the disc jockeys for playing them.

Tual, Blanchard L.

Blanchard L. Tual was the lawyer responsible for breaking Colonel Tom Parker's stranglehold on the Elvis Presley estate after Elvis' death. In May 1988, he was appointed by the Memphis probate court as legal guardian of Lisa Marie's financial interests with powers to investigate the business relationship between Elvis and the Colonel. Tual came to the conclusion that Parker had "violated his duty" to Elvis and the estate.

In a ruling based on Tual's determinations, a Memphis judge ordered that all payments to the Colonel should cease and that charges should be filed against Elvis' longtime manager. In fact, Parker would never come to court. In 1983, a settlement was reached whereby, in return for a one time payment of $2 million, the Colonel would divest himself of all Elvis-related assets and never use or mention Elvis' name again. This cleared the way for the formation of Elvis Presley Enterprises as we know it today. *(see also ELVIS AND THE COLONEL and PARKER, COLONEL TOM.)*

Tupelo Favorite Son Gift Shop

The gift shop in Elvis Presley Park in Tupelo.

Two Sevens Clash

According to the Rastafarian religion, any year in which numerically two sevens occur back to back, is one of extremely ill omen. 1977 was, of course, the year in which Elvis Presley died.

Two Thousand and One

Elvis used Richard Strauss' "Also Spake Zarathustra"—the theme from Stanley Kubrick's *2001, A Space Odyssey* as an overture to many of his seventies concerts. After his death, some of the more obsessive fans came up with the following numerology:

Month Elvis died	8
Day Elvis died	16
Year Elvis died	1977
	2001

And if that wasn't enough . . .

Day Elvis was born	8
Day Elvis died	16
Age Elvis died	42
Year Elvis was born	<u>1935</u>
	2001

So you see, it all adds up . . .

Twelve

Elvis' shoe size (U.S.).

UCLA

During his early days in Hollywood, Elvis attempted to enroll in a number of part-time courses at UCLA (the University of California, Los Angeles) to improve his basic education. His application was turned down by college officials who feared that his presence on campus might prove disruptive.

UFO

Elvis is reputed to have seen Unidentified Flying Objects on two occasions, once in Memphis and once hovering over his Los Angeles home on Peruguia Way in Bel Air. *(see also ALIENS.)*

Unit Number 6

Unit Number 6 was the Memphis Fire Department emergency response vehicle that first arrived at Graceland on the night of 16 August 1977, after Joe Esposito's 911 call stating that Elvis had collapsed.

Unseen Elvis

Hardback book, 1993. Compiled by Jim Curtain: Bullfinch Press.

A collection of over 400 colour and black and white photographs that includes previously unpublished family pictures and fan snapshots. In recent years, the quest for previously unseen pictures of Elvis became quite intense, and the discovery of a new cache of Elvis shots can more than warrant the publication of a book of this kind.

Available in bookstores.

Van Doren, Mamie

Mamie Van Doren ranked number three in Hollywood's lineup of "blonde bombshells" in the 1950s, behind Marilyn Monroe and Jayne Mansfield. In her 1987 autobiography *Playing The Field*, she makes claim to a 1957, Las Vegas affair with Elvis even though she was married to bandleader Ray Anthony at the time.

Vincent, Gene

When Bill Black and Scotty Moore first heard Gene Vincent's classic Capitol single "Be Bop A Lula" on the radio, the were quite convinced that it was Elvis moonlighting with another band, under an assumed name, and it took some convincing on Elvis' part that it wasn't.

Courtesy Michael Ochs Archives

Warhol, Andy

Painting, 1963.
Legendary pop artist Andy Warhol produced one painting of Elvis Presley. Titled *Double Elvis*, the work is a repeated image of Elvis holding a gun from the movie *Flaming Star*. The painting measures 81" by 71", with silk-screen ink and synthetic polymer paint on canvas.
The painting is owned by the Andy Warhol Estate. Reproductions, including postcards, are available from Nouvelles Images, 45700 Lombreuil, France.

Watches

Elvis watches come in all shapes, sizes and designs. Most are inexpensive, in the $30–100 range, although some of the older examples are now collectors items and extremely valuable. (These fan watches should not be confused with watches that were actually owned by Elvis which are among the most expensive watches in the world and appear now and then at auction.)
Elvis watches are available in large numbers at souvenir and jewelry stores.

WDIA

Black R&B radio station WDIA in Memphis that, in the early-to-mid-fifties, with both B.B. King and Rufus Thomas among its featured DJs, initially attempted to ban Elvis records in a piece of reverse discrimination by then programme director David James. Fortunately, both Thomas and King liked Elvis' music enough to totally ignore the ban.

West, Delbert (Sonny) and Robert (Red)

Red and Sonny West were Elvis' personal bodyguards and certainly the most famous members of the Memphis Mafia. After being fired by Vernon Presley in 1976, they co-authored the book *Elvis – What Happened? (see ELVIS – WHAT HAPPENED.)*

Andy Warhol's 1963 Double Elvis

Westmoreland, Kathy

Kathy Westmoreland, a one time runner-up in the Miss Teenage America contest, sang backup for Elvis between 1970 and 1977. Since Elvis' death, she, like so many other characters from the periphery of the legend, has attempted to forge a career as a professional "friend of Elvis," making public appearances, playing tribute shows, cutting Elvis-related records and publishing her autobiography *Elvis and Kathy* in which she claims that while dating Elvis, the two of them slept together but never had sex. She also makes the claim, supported by Larry Geller and Charlie Hodges, but denied by other Elvis intimates, that

Elvis, at the time of his death, was suffering from bone cancer and that was the reason for his massive drug use.

Elvis seemingly may not have been as devoted to Kathy as she claims. During a 1975 tour, he is on record as having repeatedly introduced her on stage with the words "this is Kathy Westmoreland. She will take affection from anybody, anytime, anyplace. In fact, she gets it from the whole band." When Ms. Westmoreland complained about this treatment, Elvis seemingly turned nasty and informed the crowd at a show in Greensboro, North Carolina: "Our soprano singer doesn't like the way I introduce her—and if she doesn't like it, she can get the hell off the stage."

Wheeler III, Treatise

Treatise Wheeler III was the drunken eighteen-year-old who, at 4 A.M. on the morning of 16 August 1977, ran his white Ford Fairlane into a crowd of Elvis mourners outside Graceland, killing two young Louisiana women, Juanita Johnson and Marie Hovatar, and injuring a third. Immediately following the incident, police were forced to rescue Wheeler from the angry crowd that was rapidly turning into a lynch mob. He was released from prison in 1983 after serving just half of a ten-year sentence.

Whiskey decanters

The early eighties saw a rash of Elvis whiskey decanters, figurines of Elvis in every phase of his career, and—a particular favourite—a white porcelain bust in which the booze was poured from the back of the King's head. The Formosa Cafe on Santa Monica Boulevard in Hollywood (right next to Warner Brothers' Hollywood studios) boasts the world's largest collection of Elvis whiskey decanters.

Elvis decanters are no longer being manufactured, but a careful scan of the top shelves in "mom and pop" liquor stores can reveal leftover decanters gathering dust, but still for sale.

White, Morning Dove

Morning Dove White, a full-blooded Cherokee Indian who died in 1835, was Elvis' great-great-great-grandmother.

Why Elvis?

Radio show circa 1990.

In the late eighties/early nineties, KALX-FM in Berkeley ran a call-in show called "Why Elvis?" on which listeners could (literally) air their feelings and theories about Elvis.

Wild At Heart

Feature film, 1990. Nicholas Cage, Laura Dern, Willem Dafoe, Diane Ladd, Harry Dean Stanton. Directed by David Lynch.

Film critic Henry Cabot Beck remarked that David Lynch's *Wild At Heart* was "what Elvis movies should have been like." Certainly actor Nicholas Cage performs a tour de force of Elvis mannerisms as a modern outlaw who treats Elvis as a kind of personal god in this bizarre and violent road movie.

Available on videocassette.

Woman Who Loved Elvis, The

TV Movie, 1994. Roseanne Arnold, Tom Arnold, Cynthia Gibb, Sally Kirkland, Danielle Harris. Directed by Ronald M. Lautore.

Roseanne Arnold, star of the long-running hit sitcom "Roseanne," stars in this made-for-TV movie that focuses on a woman in small town, blue-collar America who, after an unpleasant divorce, succumbs to near-religious Elvis mania and fills her home with Elvis artifacts. This is probably one of the best-ever dramatic studies of the almost spiritual belief that otherwise rational individuals can invest in the memory of Elvis.

Not yet available on videocassette.

Wood, Anita

Anita Wood met and dated Elvis in 1957 when she was a DJ on radio station WHHM and hosted the TV show "Top Ten Party." Wood was one of the first women to be identified in the international media as Elvis Presley's steady girlfriend, and rumour had it that Elvis and Wood planned to marry, but Colonel Tom Parker intervened, insisting that Elvis should remain single at that stage of his career. In 1977, she won a reported $240,000 settlement from a Memphis newspaper that had alleged she was still having an affair with Elvis while married to ex-Cleveland Brown's star Johnny Brewer.

Wood, Natalie

The names of Elvis and movie star Natalie Wood were romantically linked in 1956 at the time when Elvis was first in Hollywood and hanging out with Wood, Dennis Hopper, Nick Adams, and others who had previously made up the entourage of the late James Dean. Elvis and Natalie Wood dated, and in October of 1956, Elvis even took her to Memphis meet his parents. Later, she would handle disengaging from the relationship like a true professional, issuing the following public statement: "We value our friendship. We want to keep on being friends, but I dread the publicity we're getting because I know it can ruin a friendship. We're not in love. We're both eager about our careers and too young." *(see also ADAMS, NICK.)*

Elvis with Natalie Wood

Wright, Lou

According to the tabloid *The Midnight Globe*, Lou Wright had been Elvis' secret psychic from 1977 to the time of his death. After Elvis died, she further claimed to be in contact with his spirit "on the other side."